AWESOME ENCOUNTERS

Two brothers, a prominent businessman and a respected chemist, had their Sierra camping trip interrupted by huge manlike creatures ... who were desperately trying to communicate with them ...

A family in Littlerock, California, was forced to leave its house when rocks were hurled at it by unmistakable giant "men" from a nearby ridge ...

Reporters have recently come back with reliable evidence—including photographs—verifying the astonishing fact that what might have been only a legend is real! Here is the amazing truth about the footprints ... the forms glimpsed in the woods ... and the face-to-face encounters with the incredible Bigfoot!

BIGFOOT

by

B. Ann Slate

and

Alan Berry

BANTAM BOOKS · TORONTO · NEW YORK · LONDON

BIGFOOT
A Bantam Book / July 1976

ISBN 0-553-02968-1

Published simultaneously in the United States and Canada

PRINTED IN THE UNITED STATES OF AMERICA

III

*Now, as lightning pitchforked in dark pastures of
   sky
above the remote Bluff Creek wilderness,
dwindling sanctum of strange man-ape beings,
I felt a kinship with those lost hearts
beating hugely against the fall of time.*

*And as night gathered in the long canyons
I took the headlamp which would light me down
and signaled out across the miles; so, linked
at least in ceremony, Bigfoot and I moved
in separate sorrows along our evening trails.*

*As published in *Mountain Gazette*, July 1975.

Contents

a ... disappeared ... in the summer,
... I began to take food offerings and there...
soon started what Warren called "lip-smack-
teeth-popping" and spells of "wishing" that
interpreted as begging for foods. By then the

Prologue

Monster, mutant, ancient man, or migrant from another world? These are the questions being raised about the towering, hair-covered creature commonly called Bigfoot. Both in physiognomy and in his approach to man, he differs in numerous ways from the smaller, white Yeti, or Abominable Snowman of the Himalayas. While Sherpa legends and occasional glimpses of the furtive Yeti and its tracks have been documented, the contemporary and variously colored giant now emerging out of America's forests and high deserts of the West Coast has behaved more as a curious spectator and only now comes timidly closer.

This book concerns itself primarily with the most recent Bigfoot encounters in the state of California, with a special chapter on incidents in Pennsylvania which may offer a clue to the possible origin of some of these strange behemoths.

Whether Bigfoot is increasing in number or whether our constantly expanding civilization is intruding into his formerly secluded domain, is too early to determine. While there is a healthy and natural human fear of anything huge in size, combining unbelievable strength and speed, and bearing apelike inhuman features, there is also something touching in the creature's attempt at communication and, perhaps, at appealing to us for something.

The Bigfoot search is on. Although it is too soon to call him "man," latest developments indicate we may be in error by thinking him a beast.

B.A.S./A.B.

Preface
by a Bigfoot Tracker

We live in an age in which the many different frontiers of knowledge are being pushed back with unprecedented speed.

In many directions, but not in all.

The people who are doing the pushing and those who are supporting them are not generally involved by accident. Somebody is paying for the effort. If there is money to be made from such research, the resources applied can be considerable. When taxpayers provide the money, if they can be made to feel that the subject area is of vital importance, the resources available can be almost unlimited. They can be so great as to put men on the moon.

At the opposite end of this scale there are areas that do not offer a profit and that society considers a waste of time and not worthy of support. In those areas there are very few people doing the pushing and they have little with which to push.

This book deals with three such neglected areas: mainly with the reports of encounters with hairy, humanlike giants, but also with unidentified flying objects and with some aspects of what are loosely termed "psychic" phenomena.

There is no doubt that there is a relationship in the way these subjects are treated by society and the problems that face those trying to learn more about them.

"Science," meaning perhaps the majority of the scientific establishment, has no use for them. Science "knows" that there are no hairy giants, that the flying objects, if identified, would prove to be something quite ordinary, and that mind and matter conform to limitations that are generally recognized.

This general opinion does not prevent a few scientists from actively conducting research in these fields, and it probably stimulates participation by laymen who would otherwise be unable to keep up. It does, however, prevent the vast resources available to governments and large scientific institutions from being applied to such research. Progress, as a result, is bound to be slow.

For nearly twenty years I have been one of the laymen involved in investigating reports of hairy giants. As a newspaperman I tend to be skeptical about any story of something unusual, and I also have a great deal of experience in questioning people on a multitude of subjects. I have seen literally hundreds of footprints that appeared to be made by some creature similar to man but a great deal larger and heavier, and in attempting to determine what made these footprints I have talked to hundreds of people who gave convincing accounts of seeing just such a creature.

At the same time I have been unable to uncover any evidence whatever that such footprints were produced by any human agency. There have been hoaxes, of course, but the most elaborate of them have simply lacked the ability to duplicate the type of footprints for which I am seeking an explanation.

The same is true regarding the motion picture of a hair-covered giant taken in California in 1967 by Roger Patterson. Fake movies, before and since, have never withstood rigorous investigation for long, but every study of the Patterson film and every inquiry into the circumstances under which it was made have tended to confirm its authenticity.

Research into old, long forgotten records has confirmed that reports of such creatures have been continual, from the original Indian inhabitants of North America and from the explorers and fur traders who invaded the unmapped interior. And paleontology has provided evidence of likely ancestors for the giants witnesses now describe.

These are matters with which I am thoroughly familiar; I can vouch for their authenticity. Lacking any physical remains, the case for the existence of the hairy giants cannot be considered proven, but all the other evidence is there, and in quantity.

Most of this material has been gathered from a fairly limited and homogeneous area, the temperate, moist, mountainous country extending from central California through Oregon and Washington to central British Columbia. And almost without exception it fits into a single, tidy framework.

Footprints have been very similar to those of a flat-footed man, the differences, in addition to superhuman size, being mainly that the foot is considerably broader in proportion and that the toes tend to be of more uniform size. Sighting reports have described creatures completely covered with short hair, color ranging through white, grays, browns, and black. Also, they stand and walk upright, much like men, but are usually far larger and more heavily built.

These creatures, commonly called "Sasquatch" or "Bigfoot," have apelike faces, but unlike the known apes, they are good swimmers and can apparently see in the dark. They eat just about anything, including leaves and the tips of evergreen boughs. They do not use tools, weapons, fire, or clothes, nor do they have homes, but live a wandering, foraging, solitary life much like that of a bear.

Since there are relatively few sighting reports in winter and few tracks are found in snow, they may well sleep through the cold months as a bear does. Most of them, particularly females with young, are apparently much more cautious than bears about exposing themselves to humans. Being primates, they presumably have larger brains than other animals, but like gorillas, they have a way of life for which superior intelligence is not required.

The creature population in any one area appears to

be very small, and this seems to have always been the case, but the species cannot be said to be in any way endangered or even much disturbed by man's activities. If we consider their vast range, they must number in the thousands.

Man's total failure in hunting them is not so hard to understand as it might appear at first. He has no dogs that will track them, and if he did, he would be incapable of keeping up, considering their reported speed. He does not know enough about them to call and lure them in, bait them, or trap them, and because he refuses to believe that they exist, when he does stumble on one he is usually too astounded to do anything.

The creature itself is not really exceptional. It is just an upright-standing primate adapted to life in a temperate climate—man himself has those characteristics. If it is bigger than man and hair-covered, so is a gorilla. And while there are Indian traditions endowing it with psychic powers—mind reading, for instance—I have not encountered any evidence along those lines.

In all, research in the area where I have been active has roughed out the picture of a creature that presents no real problems except how to collect one. I am aware, however, that other people have found other things.

There are, for instance, footprints apparently made by feet with only three toes. These tracks have been reported, photographed, and cast both in southern California and in the eastern United States. I must confess that my attitude toward them is similar to that of most scientists toward the five-toed prints. I haven't seen one, and knowing no acceptable explanation for them, I'd just as soon forget them.

As to linking the Sasquatch with visitors from outer space, I see no need to do so. But Earth could hardly be the only inhabited planet in the universe, or man the most advanced intellect in it. Since man can travel only a relatively tiny distance into space, it seems reasonable to assume that other creatures with far greater capabilities may be flying in to look us over, especially since we started setting off atomic explosions and launching things outside Earth's atmosphere.

It is understandable, too, that when people report seeing an animal that science insists does not exist on Earth, it should be suggested that it comes from somewhere else. But the Sasquatch, as I know them, fit very logically among the other creatures of Earth— far more so than does man himself. If they have been seen near UFOs, I would prefer to consider it a coincidence or to assume that the occupants of the UFO were just looking at the Sasquatch, or vice versa.

But these are things I have chosen not to explore. The authors of this book have explored them, and knowing so well the difficulties and prejudices that they face, I cannot do otherwise than recommend that the reader give their findings full and fair consideration.

JOHN GREEN
Author of *On the Track of the Sasquatch,*
Year of the Sasquatch,
The Sasquatch File

1

Rock Giants in the Sierra

The wooded plateau might have seemed strangely vacant of animal and birdlife to the two brothers, but the warm July sun was still high as they arrived at camp, and if it seemed that the mountain glades and brushy ravines were usually quiet, it was, after all, for most wild creatures and man alike, siesta time. When they'd dropped their packs, opened the shelter where camp utensils and food provisions were stored, and finished checking out the grounds of the seasonal retreat, they stretched out on the springy pine-needle mat beneath the towering trees and napped. Only the drone of a pesky fly would disturb their slumbers for the remainder of the afternoon.

But something was different about camp that day. It was not merely their inability to flush out a single deer as they hiked in, but something had been into the shelter and had moved things about—milk cans that they'd stored foodstuffs in, sleeping bags lashed to the ceiling, and their cookware, packed in a box. Something had pried open a hole in the roof of the beaver lodgelike structure, moving limbs and branches and tearing through a plastic lining. It could be a bear, they'd guessed. Only, bears usually ransacked the shelter if they gained entry.

There was none of that here—no claw or tooth marks, shredded cardboard, or upset milkcan. It was rather as if someone had been searching for something and had jostled and undone the goods with care.

Had hippies discovered the remote campsite, located three thousand feet about the nearest roadway, a half-day's rigorous hike away? Nothing appeared to have been taken or used.

At dusk, when Warren and Lewis Johnson arose to prepare their supper over an iron boxwood stove, they were refreshed. Any vague suspicion about the camp's visitor had lapsed with their dreams; they now felt they were lucky that it hadn't been a bear.

And if the squirrels still didn't chatter and the birds still failed to warble and call, with their wood-chopping, talk, and the clanging of pots and pans the men were making enough noise on their own to fill the surrounding void. They did not even hear—rather, pay attention to—an inordinately loud crack of a dry limb or the occasional skee-runch of a footfall as the shadowy reason for it all approached; they had no reason to suspect anything except that a rotten limb had broken off a tree, as rotten limbs will, and that a deer, curious as deer sometimes are, was cautiously observing their activity.

It was the first week in July 1971. They could not have guessed that within the next few hours the course of their lives would be changed forever.

Indians native to the region had called it Che-halum'che, meaning "rock giant"; these were the northern Miwok, an ancient people who ground acorns for several millennia on slabs of rock lining the Stanislaus River, on the western slope of the Sierra Nevada in California. To the southern Miwok, along the banks of the Merced River in Yosemite, it was Oo'le, also meaning "rock giant." Across the San Joaquin Valley to the west, around Mt. Tamalpais, the Miwok of the coastal hills called it Loo-poo-oi'yes, and among those tribes farther north, living around what is now called Clear Lake, it was known as Olayome. As with their Sierra brethren, both Loo-poo-oi'yes and Olayome were rock giants. And they were nocturnal. And they lived in caves. And they made a crying noise, hoo-oo-oo, like a baby to lure the Miwok away from the safety of their fires. And they especially liked Miwok women, to eat—at least, according to legend.

But the Johnson brothers—Warren, forty-two, a business executive and a family man, and Lewis, thirty-two, an expert in chemical processes used in sugar refining—had no knowledge of the legend as it was recorded nearly three quarters of a century earlier by naturalist C. Hart Merriam.[1] Even if they'd stumbled across it in their occasional readings about the area, they would have had little reason to recall it up until now. They'd hunted deer, bear, and grouse on the slopes surrounding the old Basque sheepherders' camp for years, and the region and nearly everything that inhabited it were as familiar as a fence line and life within one's backyard.

Even if they'd known the legend, they would have scoffed at the Indians' foolish superstitions and beliefs. They did not believe in northern California's so-called Bigfoot. They'd heard of it, all right. They thought the mountain folk of California's northern quarter took their drink a mite too seriously. Had they read the local newspapers, they would have known that some of the local mountain folk took their drink seriously as well.

Like one old-timer who'd been cutting firewood near Cold Springs off the Sonora Highway late in the afternoon of January 27, 1963. He didn't want to give his name. He just wanted to leave a message: he'd just seen a hairy manlike monster, and it had nearly frightened him to death.

The Tuolumne County Sheriff's Department took the call. The clerks and deputies on duty at the office in

Sonora that night had a good laugh about it. But they responded. Perhaps it was something in the caller's voice. In a news account a day later, the man was quoted by a deputy, "You'll think I'm crazy and put me in a straitjacket." He said that he had just seen a man who stood between nine and ten feet tall in the road by a gravel pit where he'd been cutting wood.

"It was moving around. It appeared to be human but was the most awful thing I've ever seen. . . .

"I'm scared. I'm an adult and I'm not crazy. I'm not drunk. I don't even drink."

The caller had been so distraught, a deputy recalled, that he'd refused to talk anymore over the phone and had passed it to a friend, to vouch for his sanity and the fact that something strange had really happened.

It was 8:30 P.M. Deputy Sheriff William "Bill' Huntley, later to become a lieutenant, chief of detectives, and a candidate for sheriff, rolled on the call. Huntley guessed that whoever the caller was, and it was never learned, he'd probably tippled too much at a local tavern or he'd seen a bear and his imagination had taken flight.

At Strawberry Resort he met with Elbert Miller, a resident deputy who lived near Cold Springs and knew the area. Miller, in a part-time job with the state Department of Water Resources, in the course of thirty years had snowshoed and skied some thirty thousand miles through the High Sierra doing snow surveys. He knew the mountains like few men ever get to know them. He was equally incredulous of the report.

The men had a cup of hot coffee and braced themselves against the freezing night air before leaving the resort. Like Warren and Lewis Johnson, eight and one-half years later, not twenty-five miles from where the deputies sat in the coffee shop, they did not believe in northern California's Bigfoot creature, or in any monster at all.

It was at the Cold Springs gravel pit, within the hour, that Huntley's and Miller's worlds would begin to crumble and disintegrate in the face of a different reality. There was no bargaining with it; they would never be quite the same in their outlook on life again.

"There was definitely some creature in the woods," Huntley later told the Sonora *Union Democrat*.[2] "I've never heard anything like it."

Miller would say, "I've never heard a sound like that in all my years in the woods."

The creature had cried out and screamed from the dark brushy thickets when the law officers arrived at the gravel-pit site. Huntley, ten years later, recalled that he and Miller had parked their patrol car in a clearing near the pit, thinking they would get out, look around, find nothing, and then leave, having done their duty. They got out, he said. The air was cold. The ground was frozen solid. They stepped to the edge of some bushes and relieved themselves. Suddenly, as they were about to return to the car, from not more than twenty or thirty yards on the other side of it there was a horrible cry.

"My hair stood on end," Huntley said. "I immediately ran and opened the trunk of the car and grabbed the shotgun. The thing screamed again, and it was real close. We didn't know what it was or what was going to happen. . . ."

They jumped into the car, rolled up the windows, and tried to beam a spotlight on it. But the creature was somewhere in the heavy undergrowth concealed from view.

"It began circling us, all the time making these weird sounds, like maybe a deaf-mute would make. . . ."

They thought perhaps it was a deaf-mute or a human in some kind of horrible agony. They even called to it, and it responded with calls of its own. But its behavior didn't seem human at all.

"First it was here, then there—maybe fifty yards from where we'd just heard it," Deputy Miller recalled. "And no nothing between, no sounds of running or crashing through the brush or anything. The jack pine is thick through there. I don't see how it could do it, any human . . . and it moved with incredible speed."

When the "monster" seemed to move away down into a canyon, the deputies returned to Strawberry. They wanted witnesses. They recruited a resort employee.

Back near the pit, this time on the main highway, they again encountered the creature. They stopped the car. In Sonora, thirty miles away, a radio dispatcher monitored the scene as Huntley spoke, "It's heading toward the car. Here it comes. . . . Now it seems to be circling the car. It sounds more and more like an animal of some kind. . . .

"It's definitely not a bear. Elbert [Miller] thinks it's more possibly a mountain lion . . . but it's not a mountain-lion noise. . . ."

The noise was, Huntley maintained, "like a human in distress."

Whatever the creature was, they failed to see it. At the same time, neither the patrol car's spotlight nor their shouts frightened it away. When it finally left, its cries fading off into the forest, it seemed to leave of its own volition.

Later, Huntley made an appeal to the unidentified phone callers through the media,[3] "If we could get these people to come in or call and tell us just what they did see, we could make a lot more sensible approach to this thing. We would listen with reason and wouldn't put them in a straitjacket. If they did see a thing of this description, it's important to the community, the sheriff's office, and everyone concerned. . . ."

Nine to ten feet tall and hair-covered. "It appeared to be human, but it was the most awful thing I've ever seen," the eyewitness had said.

How many people had seen such a creature, had come across its footprints, had heard it in the night, or had otherwise known of its presence prior to this incident? The mystery callers never came forward. Their fear of ridicule and embarrassment was and is commonplace. Who would believe anyone who said seriously that he had nearly been scared to death by a hairy giant?

But a precedent was set. Only a month later, a seemingly intrepid pilot reported sighting a ten-foot-tall creature on the ground in the vicinity of Confidence, near Sonora.

And the following month, a couple honeymooning at a ski lodge near Cold Springs would ask the lodge owner about a hair-covered creature they'd just seen that stood between eight and nine feet tall. The lodge owner had calmly replied that the same creature had been seen before, there was nothing to be alarmed about!

So it would be, unbeknownst to the Johnson brothers only a few years later, in 1971, as they hunkered down warming their hands before a fire in their camp only a few miles away, to the southeast.

But '63 was the year the big-footed rock giants (the "Terror of the Tuolumnes," as one San Francisco newspaper called them) would make headlines from the midrift recesses of California's rugged Sierra. In December, another report leaked out: Deputy Elbert Miller, a backwoods lawman with thirty years' snow-survey experience in some of the Sierra's wildest regions, was back in the limelight, this time following a creature track near Strawberry Resort, where only months before he and others had first met up with the ancient Miwok legend come to life and had laughed and joked about a frightened woodcutter's strange report.

There was no laughing and joking now. Something with a very big foot and a superlong stride had left hundreds of footprints in the snow along the abandoned Old Strawberry Road before wandering down the steep, heavily wooded mountainside toward the Stanislaus River. The footprints measured nearly twice the length of Miller's bootprints. The step between impressions averaged about two and one-half times that of his own. There were no other tracks or impressions in the shallow but new-fallen snow.

Ken Sneed, owner of the Strawberry Resort, who'd recently retired from Douglas Aircraft Company after twenty years as an accident investigator, had joined the investigation at Miller's request. Miller had asked him to carry a gun.

"There were two to three inches of fresh snow on the road," he recalled. "We hadn't gone very far from where we came on the trail when I suddenly turned around and it dawned on me, here I am taking two steps to every stride—hey, what the hell is this?"

Sneed estimated the footprint length at sixteen inches, the stride, from seven to eight feet. Although the prints appeared as if made by moccasins, each revealed five distinct toe impressions; whatever had made them, evidently it was accustomed to barefoot travel.

After he and Miller had followed the track for several hundred yards, they discovered a second set of similar prints coming down off the embankment above the road.

"I kept looking around for any evidence of how they could have been made," Sneed said. "Whoever or whatever, you'd think we'd have seen or known who it was . . . because they were humanlike tracks."

In the end, the contradictions that faced the veteran investigator of aircraft-crash causes proved to be too much to bear. Where the two tracks left the road and disappeared through the trees in the canyon below, the men stopped. It was getting dark, and they were feeling more and more uneasy.

"Whatever it was, it was big," Sneed said. "I sure as hell wasn't going to go down into the canyon, even with a .357 magnum and him with a .38 special!"

Deputy Miller had similar problems dealing with the reality. On one hand, he was certain the footprints were hoaxed. He said he kept trying to imagine someone rolling an enormous bicyclelike wheel with fake feet attached to it. "But there wasn't any evidence . . . they'd have had to have been suspended from a helicopter, and that didn't make any sense because the tracks didn't just go down the road in a straight line, they wandered up and down the hill on either side, through the trees and everywhere."

On the other hand, he said, "We had a guy up here

about that time, a tall athletic guy—he might have been out running there. . . ."

And in an interview ten years later: "I never did satisfy in my mind how they were made."

A human jogger barefoot in the snow? At the Strawberry Resort, longtime employees will tell you that such strange discoveries as the footprints, the eerie sounds at night, and reports of monster sightings are not uncommon. The word travels quickly through the mountain communities. But it's seldom publicized. Few people care to risk possible embarrassment and ridicule through public exposure.

Perhaps no one felt more ill-at-ease with the reports that did leak out to the press in the '60s than the county sheriff. Guessing the potential for fear and panic among the county populace, he at first derided the reports as the work of a hermit who wore a bearskin coat and enjoyed frightening people. Later, it was the work of a "squeak owl." "I've heard them follow me when I was alone in the woods, and it's enough to scare a person to death if he doesn't know what it is. You think you hear something and you look over your shoulder, and you could swear it's right behind you in the shadows. You say, 'Hi,' and it'll say, 'Hi!' right back. But it's just a squeak owl . . . used to have a lot of them around in these mountains, and I think they're making a comeback."

In January 1968, Robert James, Jr., and Leroy Larwick, both of the Sonora area, claimed to have buzzed their plane to within fifty feet of a hairy creature that stood ten to twelve feet tall.

In November 1969, Mike Scott, twenty-six, a logger, reportedly leveled the sights of a high-powered rifle on a Bigfoot-Rock Giant near the Calaveras Big Trees National Park and pumped three rounds into it at a distance of thirty yards.

The creature fled, according to an eyewitness, running away uphill on two legs, leaving a trail of blood. Scott and the witness also fled, and no one returned to the scene until the trail was cold.

In June 1970, Wes Chormicle of Santa Barbara, an

outdoors-equipment salesman, and a Ventura College student friend followed the path of a creature that had a fourteen- to sixteen-inch foot and a four-foot stride for about six miles, in the Bailey Ridge area of northeastern Yosemite National Park.

In July 1970, a deputy sheriff reported finding an eighteen-inch-long footprint in a mudflat beside a small lake near Mammoth, California, on the eastern slope of the Sierra about one hundred miles southeast of the Cold Springs sighting area.

In late October 1970, Ni Orsi, a former Olympic skiier, and a friend found the fresh track of a creature whose foot was sixteen to eighteen inches long, near Ebbets Pass on Highway 4, about fifty miles northeast of Cold Springs. There were six inches of snow on the road, which had been closed hours before, and it was still snowing. The creature had crossed from side to side only moments ahead of their vehicle.

In September 1971, a sheriff's lieutenant reported sighting an eight-foot-tall hair-covered creature southeast of Mammoth.

Northward, but southeast of Lake Tahoe, in July 1973, two couples vacationing from Utah, driving up the old Kingsbury Grade, watched in frightened awe as a seven- to eight-foot-tall hair-covered creature with a leathery but humanlike face stood up beside the road and walked away into the timber and brush. Sheriff's deputies later told them that the creature had frightened two young women driving a car just ahead of them and that there had been other reports. The deputies said not to be alarmed, for it was just "a crazy Indian."[4]

Southshore show-biz? In July 1965, Dr. Robert W. Denton of Bishop, California, was camping with a group of Boy Scouts near the Minarets, just west of Mammoth. A pack mule tethered in a boggy area kicked up a portion of a skull. It was a humanlike skull (the calvarium), only it was unusually large and massive.

Dr. Denton brought the skull out and sent it to Dr. Gerald K. Ridge, Ventura County Pathologist, for analysis and possible identification.

A few weeks later, Dr. Ridge wrote Dr. Denton, explaining that he had turned the specimen over to two scientists at the University of California as Los Angeles, who'd expressed great interest in it and were seeking information as to exactly where it was found.

The skull, Dr. Ridge said, had some remarkable features. For one thing, it was unusually long for a human skull. For another, the nuchal ridge in the occipital zone (the "knot" at the back of one's head) was exceptionally high. Neither of the UCLA scientists had ever observed such a high nuchal ridge in their studies of modern man, including Indian, Ridge said; and neither had he, himself, in all his years as a pathologist.

The feature was so remarkable, he said, that he'd wondered whether the skull was actually that of some *"anthropoid species other than human."*

Perhaps the most remarkable thing about this skull was that it mysteriously disappeared. Today neither man—one is in Arizona, the other in Chicago—has any idea of the extraordinary specimen's whereabouts, and indeed, one even denies ever having seen and handled it.

Meanwhile, though they had no knowledge of the Miwok legend or of the occasional evidence of the Bigfoot-Rock Giant creatures as it has emerged in the Sierra in recent years, it was against such a background that Warren and Lewis Johnson were situated that July 1971 evening, on a high volcanic plateau once coveted by sheepherders, in a wooded ravine, before the glowing embers of their dying cookfire.

They'd had a cup of tea and talked before retiring to bed in the beaver lodge shelter. There'd been a few scraps of broiled Spam left over from dinner. They were left in place on a wire grill atop the box stove for a breakfast snack, if some hungry animal didn't snatch them up first.

An animal would come to take the scraps, but it wasn't quite like any animal they'd ever imagined or expected.

"It was just after dark," Warren Johnson recalled. "We'd bedded down inside the shelter and had turned the lantern off when . . . suddenly all hell broke loose down in the camp kitchen, about twenty yards away.

"There's an old bear up there that we'd see every couple of years. This was the first thing that crossed our minds—that he'd come into camp looking for food.

"But then, with all the clatter of pots and pans and utensils being tossed about, there was this weird snarling and snorting. It was a blowing sound, and there was something like teeth popping, and finally a violent sound like somebody was out there and was screaming and beating his chest, an awfully big chest.

"We knew then that it wasn't any bear, and it scared us. All we had between us was a .22 revolver I'd packed along. From the sounds it was making, whatever was out there just wasn't the kind of thing you'd take a shot at in the dark with a .22. It sounded like it easily could have torn the shelter apart if it had a mind to. . . ."

When the commotion finally ended and they thought they could hear the thing crashing off through the brush and trees leaving the area, they pushed back the upright log door of the shelter and, with flashlights and the .22 in hand, cautiously emerged.

What they saw completely unnerved them. The "kitchen," consisting of the stove, their various utensils for cooking, and a small store of bagged and canned food, was a shambles. Some pots and pans had been hurled as far as fifty feet in different directions. Other items were scattered everywhere, it seemed.

They'd heard it all happen, and this much wasn't a great surprise. It was the footprints that turned up in their flashlight beams: enormous, five-toed footprints that looked almost human yet spoke of something at least twice the size of either of the brothers!

"I can't describe the feeling," Warren said. "Suddenly we got scared all over again. Oh, we'd heard about this Bigfoot thing—I guess I'd read about in a magazine several years before, but neither of us ever talked about it or were the least bit interested. But there the prints were, and we'd listened to it crashing around . . . there was no other rational explanation.

"It seemed like we both got the same feeling at the same time. It was like we knew that the thing really hadn't left and that it was out there somewhere watching us. We tore back uphill to the shelter and got inside, and pulled the log in, and lashed it to the roof beams. We didn't know what was going to happen, but we weren't about to take any more chances. That shelter was all we had!"

It turned out that they were correct: the creature hadn't gone far, and it returned, this time to walk and skulk about the shelter close enough that they could hear its breathing. Once it pushed and pulled at the logs and branches and shook a loose end of the black plastic tarpaulin lining. Then it backed off and could be heard again down in the kitchen area, where it snorted and growled and finally let go with a bellowing cry accompanied with more of the chest-beating.

"It was awful—the most frightening sound I've ever heard from that close up," Warren said. "It was like the thing was telling us he was the meanest creature in the woods—really antagonistic and belligerent—and I want to tell you, we believed it! He had no brief with either of us. We weren't about to argue. . . ."

Shocked beyond measure, terrified by thoughts of what might happen if the creature decided to investigate the contents of the shelter, the brothers had crouched down, listened, imagined, and prayed for the thing to leave. And it did, finally, though they spent most of the night awake and wondering if it would return yet a third time.

But daylight reality had softened the effect of the night before. Though they talked of abandoning the camp permanently, curiosity began to take hold. They wondered whether they shouldn't attempt to investigate, to learn something more about their frightening but oddly cautious visitor. More and more, it seemed that the violence was impersonal, the threatening sounds more bluff than bite. When they eventually backpacked out of the area and returned to their homes in the valley, they knew they could not leave the mystery alone.

It was the beginning of an odyssey. They had already

taken the first inadvertent step on a road without any
obvious beginning and with no apparent end, and no
way to turn back. There was no denying the footprints
—casts would establish their physical occurrence; on
later trips, with the aid of tape recorders, there would
be no denying the strange creature's vocalizations and
sounds. But where would the footprints lead them? What
message might there be in the sounds? Would they ever
see the remarkable Bigfoot creatures who walked in the
night? In the Miwok legend, the giants relished human
flesh. What did the Bigfoot-Rock Giants want that for
the first time in modern times they would so boldly approach a human camp?

NOTES

Preface. John Green, *The Sasquatch File,* Cheam Publishing
   Ltd. (Agassiz, B.C., 1973).

1. C. Hart Merriam, *Weird Tales of the Mewan Indians*
   (Cleveland, The Arthur H. Clark Co., 1910).

2. "Report: 10-foot Shrieking Monster," *The Union Democrat*
   (Sonora, Calif., January 28, 1963).

3. "The Mountain Monster: Jest or Giant?" *The Union Democrat* (Sonora, Calif., January 29, 1963).

4. "Bigfoot Sighted?" Letters, *The Evening Gazette* (Reno, Nevada, August 11, 1973).

2

Dialogue with Bigfoot

When Warren and Lewis Johnson returned to the Sierra camp two weeks later, they were better armed to protect themselves, and they carried cameras and tape recorders to obtain evidence. They also took along Warren's son, Larry, twenty-three; Bill McDowell, a building contractor and family friend; and a fifth man, another family friend who was mountainwise and could, the others joked, "hunt bear with a switch." All of the men were familiar with the camp region, having slept out and hunted there for years; all shared a certain anticipation and excitment, especially Larry, Bill, and the fifth man, for they knew that Warren and Lewis were not given to practical jokes or telling tall tales. To friends, acquaintances, and business associates, the brothers were regarded as men of integrity and moral repute. If they said that giant creatures had turned up in the camp area, then that was probably the case.

But none of the men, including the brothers, really

expected a second encounter, perhaps least of all the fifth man, who was more apprehensive about the idea than anybody could have guessed. To him giants were creatures of Biblical yore. When, as soon as it got dark, the creatures came in, his emotional defenses seemed to crumble. He was a tall, lean man with rough-hewn features, and he was in excellent physical condition. As he and the others had huddled in the shelter while the creatures made menacing sounds nearby, he'd suddenly jumped up and declared that he was going to make a run for it—about twelve miles through the woods, to safety. He had to be forcibly restrained. Then he lapsed into a state of apparent shock, whimpering like a child and shaking convulsively most of the night.

"He was the last person any of us thought would have a problem," Warren remarked. "But it's a pretty hairy thing. Some people can't take it."

Today the incident is viewed with humor, even by the man involved, but the serious side of it has not been forgotten. The man, who looked mean enough to hunt bear with a switch, has not slept overnight in the mountains since. None of the men, in fact, now ventures into the area alone or sleeps outside the camp shelter, as had been a habit on warm nights in the past.

Encounters with the strangely vocal creatures continued to occur as the season progressed that year, and what had been a simple retreat and hunting camp soon changed into more of a frontier outpost. The eight-foot-high, fifteen-foot-diameter shelter was reinforced with new logs and timbers. Barrels for the storage of food and equipment were added. A new iron box cookstove was brought in on horseback. A corral was fashioned. Another member was added: Ron Moorehead, a nonhunter friend of McDowell's who offered to take charge of camp cooking.

Aside from the eventual participation of one of the authors, Alan Berry, late the following year, Moorehead would be the only addition to the Johnson party. Not that Warren had not invited others to join, or that scientists and investigators did not have an opportunity. Among institutions he approached were the National

Geographic Society and the Department of Anthropology at the University of California, Berkeley. The words of one anthropologist, however, seemed to sum up the general scientific attitude: "He said that even if you discovered one [Bigfoot] it would be considered just a freak of nature," Warren recalled. He'd also approached the Society for the Investigation of the Unexplained, in Columbia, New Jersey,[1] by comparison a less conservative source of scientific counsel. The society invited him to send more information and keep it advised on developments, but offered no direct help.

Finally, Warren appealed to adventurer-journalist Peter Byrne, who was then setting up a Bigfoot research center[2] at The Dalles, Oregon. But when his letters throughout the spring and summer of 1972 failed to elicit an enthusiastic response on Byrne's part, he abandoned the effort. He had not sought publicity, and neither he nor the others wanted publicity, they said, short of their success in obtaining "proof" of the creatures, photographically or otherwise. It was a fluke that Alan Berry, then writing for a small northern California daily newspaper several hundred miles away, ever came in touch with the group.

Alan had learned of Johnson through an incredulous Peter Byrne,[3] who, so long as his name wasn't involved, seemed willing enough to have a newsman look into the story.

After talking with Warren over the phone, Alan arranged a personal interview with the group at Warren's home. This took place in late July 1972, a few weeks after the group had reached a peak in their relationship with the Bigfoot family, according to Warren's report. From what the businessman Bigfoot devotee said, the group had succeeded in coaxing the creatures to take food offerings, only to have the rapport and trust dissolve suddenly, apparently as the result of some tainted luncheon meat that had been left out. The creatures had sulked afterward, it seems, then apparently had abandoned the area.

To a newsman chasing down an offbeat and bizarre story, it was only to be expected that the creatures

would inexplicably disappear just as he arrived on the
scene. It was an old and familiar development.

Warren, however, wasn't aware of Alan's credentials
when he first laid out the tale. He hadn't asked for
them. He'd assumed Alan was assisting Byrne, and
when Alan finally informed him of his newspaper tie,
he was disappointed and angry—as much with himself
as with Alan, it seemed. In deference to his sincerity
about not wanting publicity, Alan assured him that the
entire matter would remain confidential. On this basis,
the interview date was set.

Greg Lyon,[4] a close friend and colleague, accompanied Alan. As the men claimed to have recorded
Bigfoot's "voice," and as Bigfoot's voice was practically
unheard of in most Bigfoot reports except for an occasional "scream," Alan and Greg assumed that the
chance of hoax was high and planned the interview
accordingly. Alan would be the "good guy" with the
soft questions and sympathetic manner, while Greg
would be the "bad guy" with the hard questions and
disbelieving manner; and if it were possible without
arousing their suspicions, they would question the men
separately as well as in a group. The divide-and-interro-
gate whipsaw technique was not unlike one commonly
employed by police and crime investigators. If the men
could be led to alter or elaborate on the details of the
story at the interviewers' beckoning, it could be reason-
ably assumed that the story was a fabrication, to be
treated as such.

As it happened, however, the men could not be
tripped up, either separately or as a group. While their
material evidence, chiefly photographs of footprints and
tapes of admittedly unusual vocalizations and sounds,
appeared suspect, their story seemed to hold together.
If there was any deviation or flaw in the telling, it was
merely what seemed natural and honest, a candid and
usually spontaneous recall of real impressions and
events past.

There was Greg's interrogation of Lewis regarding
an alleged sighting, the only close-up view of one of the
creatures any of the men could report.

They were in the living room of Warren's modest three-bedroom tract home. Lewis, in jeans, polished boots, and flannel shirt, sat at one end of a sofa. Larry, in slacks and pressed Western-style long-sleeve shirt, sat in the middle, and Bill McDowell, similarly attired, at the other end. Warren, in knit shirt and slacks, sat in a lounge chair to one side. Greg and Alan sat, at their own insistence, on the carpeted floor, facing the others across a coffee table.

They'd been questioning the men for about an hour. Compared with the rest, Lewis seemed ill-at-ease, volunteering little except when asked. He sat back with his legs crossed. The toe of his boot bounced nervously. When Greg asked him about the sighting, Lewis avoided looking at him directly as it seemed he had done from the start. His round, thinly lined face was almost expressionless.

"Well?" Greg insisted.

Lewis sighed and threw his head back, then leaned forward, putting both feet on the floor, clasping his hands in front of him and resting his elbows on his knees. He looked at Greg seriously. "They came in," he said. "I don't remember exactly what happened, but they'd been making all this noise, and they—" He glanced at Warren, then at Bill. "Was this the time four of them . . . ?" Both men nodded. "Anyway," Lewis continued, "they had us surrounded. Then they left, and we heard this whistle."

"And one of them came back," Warren interjected.

"Yeah. Well we had peepholes in the sides of the shelter so we could look out, and we'd been watching at least forty-five minutes and all of a sudden this thing came into the area where I was looking. It came out of the timber, and I really didn't see it until it came out and crossed in the moonlight—there was moonlight shining through the trees. When I saw it, I hollered at Larry. He was looking out on the same side I was. And as I yelled the thing turned and appeared to look straight at us, and then, it spun around on one foot and went back into the timber. And that was it."

"Can you describe it?" Greg asked.

"All I could tell, it was tall. We don't know how tall. We tried to figure it out because the head was above the brush. It looked like it was about eight or ten feet tall."

"But what did it *look* like?" Greg asked.

"It was just a big shadow."

"A dark shape?"

"But it wasn't black."

"What color? Dark? Light?"

"It appeared to be a brown, it wasn't black but it stood out a little."

"Light brown?"

"It's possible."

"What else? What'd you see of its . . ."

Greg's questions were terse and rapid, running almost ahead of Lewis' responses. Lewis appeared to be trying to remember and his answers came in equally rapid spurts. But he couldn't seem to recall the details Greg was after. The frustration flashed in his eyes.

Bill McDowell interrupted, saying calmly, "Just describe the features you could make out, Lewis."

"Well, it was wide-shouldered, maybe three to four feet wide, and it was walking upright—"

"Straight up, stooped over, or what?" Greg asked.

"Well—naw, I can't say that. When you see something like that . . . I could tell it was walking upright and that it was tall, and that it was big, when it turned and ran. But it was an impression, and now I can't even remember seeing arms."

"When it turned and ran, did it stoop over?"

"Naw, it just spun around and faced us from what I could tell, and then it . . . it was just for a split second . . . then it turned and went back the way it came."

Warren again interrupted sympathetically. "I remember you saying that the thing was ugly-looking."

Lewis glanced at him. "It was moonlight, that's all I could go by," he said.

"There was another thing that you haven't mentioned," Warren said. "You said it looked like it didn't have a neck."

"Well, if it had a neck, it was a very short one."

Larry, sitting with one arm stretched out across the back of the sofa, had watched Lewis and Greg like players at a tennis match. Now Greg caught Larry's eye. "What about you? What did you see?"

The swarthy, square-jawed man smiled as if bemused. "I just had a glimpse of it," he answered. "Just movement. I couldn't make out anything. I was looking the other way and didn't have as much of a view as Lewis had from where he was watching."

"What about the color?"

"I couldn't say. All I saw was movement, something moving."

It was an excellent opportunity for Larry to corroborate Lewis' story. As Greg and Alan later compared notes, they felt that he had corroborated it, as only one telling the truth can. In fact, Lewis' very reluctance to venture beyond what he was certain that he saw and remembered, and his calm and firm insistence about the details as he recalled them, seemed to underline his credibility. If he'd wanted to elaborate on his memory or imagining, Warren had given him the opportunity. As it came off, with Warren's mention of impressions told earlier and now apparently ignored or forgotten, it seemed inconceivable that Lewis had been dishonest in his representation. Even to his remark that he couldn't remember seeing arms. Who would have remembered more, or less, of a fleeting figure seen on a dark moonlit night?

In all, the interview had lasted nearly five hours. Alan and Greg had gone over experience after experience and detail after detail, sometimes several times in an effort to catch the men off guard. But it became apparent that the men were not *on* guard. There seemed to be no bottom to their extraordinary tale, only further experiences to be recalled, analyzed, and reflected upon. In its complexity alone, Greg and Alan felt that it could not be a hoax. Yet the creature footprints they'd seen, if they were what the photos suggested, appeared static, as if made by something rigid rather than fleshy and flexible like a human foot. The tape-recorded sounds were even more suspiciously enigmatic: oddly rapid, almost-articulate vocalizations that resembled an Oriental language. Could they be those of a human voice, electronically manipulated perhaps, and recorded at other-than-normal speeds? The men were not unaware of their interviewers' doubts, and they candidly admitted that for a long time they'd found such evidence hard to accept, as well. The problem was, they explained, the footprints and sounds were real.

By the end of the evening, Greg and Alan arrived at the same conclusion: the answer lay in the camp. Would they be taken there?

As Warren had explained over the phone, he and the others were concerned about the creatures' apparent absence from the area. The group had decided not to return to camp for a few weeks, he said. Maybe if it were left alone for a while the creatures would come back or get over being "mad." The group could make no promises, Warren said. But would Greg and Alan want to go in even though there was no assurance that anything would happen?

A dialogue had been initiated, assuming all was as it seemed to be to the men. Not a verbal exchange of ideas and information certainly, but an exchange nonetheless, a reciprocal communication of sense and feeling. It had begun, inadvertently, it seems, with the creature who'd spilled the teapot, apparently scalding itself. It had thrown a violent-sounding fit after the first explosive cry of surprise and pain. "I think he blamed us for the accident," Warren said. "I don't think we would have ever known they were there, had the one not harmed itself."

Had he and Lewis witnessed a surprise Bigfoot tantrum? It seems that the enraged creature had levied responsibility on anything and everything within reach or sight, including the men in the shelter. Pots and pans had flown, then the creature had stormed around the perimeter of the shelter, snorting and growling as if it had every intent to eat the men alive. Surely it was big enough (eighteen-inch-long footprints) to have torn the shelter apart. Yet from what the men had heard, it had merely jostled the branches and logs. Having involuntarily opened its mouth, had it merely wanted to bluster and fume like a child angry with itself? When no sound came from the humans inside the shelter, had curiosity prevailed? Had the thing made a self-discovery of power, realizing that so long as the humans were walled in, it could make noise and walk through their camp as it pleased? Whatever the case, a discovery of some sort of new purpose was evident, for the creature returned a second night in the company of others of its kind.

According to Warren and Lewis, the several creatures had scrapped among themselves. There were moments when the commotion outside sounded like a barroom brawl, from the body blows, screeches, and cries. It was both amusing and terrifying, they said, for whatever the creatures were doing, it seemed obvious that it was for the men's benefit. Having been accidentally "discovered" in the area, did they stage the violent-sounding performance to frighten the men away? If this were their intent, it had an opposite effect. While Warren and Lewis had been frightened, to be sure, the obvious lack of physical violence toward them convinced them that despite the snarls and growls the creatures meant them no harm. By the time they'd finally hiked out of camp, their curiosity was running well ahead of any fear. Who were these big-footed beings? they wondered. The things jabbered a lot. Did they have a language? Could they be taught to talk? Could the men make friends with them? Would they accept food or other items? What did they look like? Would they still be around in a week or two?

The creatures were around, and seemed to remain in the general area of the camp for the remainder of the season. And as time and the weekend encounters progressed, the men's outwardly casual acceptance of their presence there, along with their refusal to be frightened off, began to pay off, it seemed.

"Toward the end of the year they seemed to become less and less ferocious," Warren said. "There were fewer growls and the chest-beating sort of thing, and more of the chatter, almost like they were really attempting to talk with us and communicate."

When the creatures reappeared early in the summer of 1972, they'd begun to take food offerings and there was even more chatter, what Warren called "lip-smacking" and "teeth-popping," and spells of "whining" that the men interpreted as begging for food. By then the men were "talking" back in attempts to coax the creatures in, within their view and camera range—for it seemed that they'd quickly retreated to the periphery once it became evident that the men were no longer terribly frightened by their presence. Little by little they were responding. There were even occasions, Warren said, when, instead of immediately falling silent when one of the men emerged from the shelter, they would continue to vocalize and carry on.

Slowly but surely the "let's make friends" tack was working, it seemed. At least until one night a package of tainted luncheon meat was left out as an offering. One of the creatures had taken the meat and buried it partially, leaving behind an enormous handprint on the ground.

The men were amused and had taken photographs of the print, but had left the spoiling meat in place. The following day they found it had been dug up and removed. As the wrapper was never found, they had no way of knowing whether the meat was eaten. They could only guess that the creatures must have taken offense, for they did not come in and vocalize that night, nor would they talk to the men on the next trip into camp, though they were heard walking in the area. On the succeeding trip, it seemed as if they'd abandoned the camp and men altogether.

This then was about the time that Greg Lyon and Alan Berry interviewed Warren, Lewis, Larry, and Bill McDowell at Warren's home, and incidentally had noted an old-hat nonchalance about the Bigfoot subject on the part of Warren's wife and youngest children. Greg and Alan would like to visit the camp, whether the creatures had departed or not, they told the men.

It seemed that there had to be some evidence there, even old evidence, that would provide a clue to the mystery. "Keep in touch," Warren had said. "We won't promise that we'll take you in, but we'll consider the idea if there's an opportunity."

Alan kept in touch. He found out that there were other, separate stories in the mid-Sierra region that tended to corroborate the Johnson tale. He made preliminary efforts to have the Bigfoot tapes and other evidence analyzed scientifically. He also made a point of getting to know the men better.

Then one evening in September, he talked over the phone with Bill McDowell, who'd just returned from several days at the camp. "I've got good news," Bill said. "Biggie is back. It looks like there's a chance you'll get to come in with us." A call to Warren confirmed the news. Alan made tentative plans. But Greg was not invited, Bill said. He and the others felt that one newsman type was enough, and at that, they had no way of knowing what effect another "stranger" in camp would have on the creatures. The previous fall, when Ron Moorehead was first brought in, the creatures had stayed away. It wasn't until Moorehead's third trip that the creatures apparently "accepted" him.

They made the trip the first weekend in October and found the camp empty of any creatures or unusual activity. But on the basis of a growing trust in the men, and old footprints shown Alan, one set of which crossed a sandy ridge a half-mile from camp, he returned for a second, two-night stay the following weekend. It was then, even as Warren and the rest of the party had cautioned a sympathetic but die-hard skeptic, that nearly everything previously described suddenly began happening in the skeptic's presence.

They had gone through the routine of pretending to close camp and bed down for the night inside the shelter. Outside, the woods were dark except where moonlight shone through the trees, filling gaps and openings. While sitting before the cookstove, they'd heard a few heavy footfalls and branches breaking.

Warren and the others, Bill McDowell and Lewis that night, had expressed a mutual sentiment that the creatures were "around" and that it was time to go into the shelter and let them come near.

Inside the thick-walled shelter, they lay side by side, quietly stretched out on sleeping bags. Alan pushed the record buttons of his tape recorder, whose microphone was attached to a tree trunk outside aimed at the woods uphill. Warren, Lewis, and Bill also had portable cassette recorders set up and aimed in other directions.

About fifteen minutes passed and the only noise heard was the hum of Alan's tape recorder and shallow breathing. Alan was tired from the long hike in. His eyes had closed and interest had begun to flag with thoughts of sleep. All of a sudden, however, outside, somewhere uphill, there was a loud, piercing whistle. With eyes now open wide in the darkness, Alan raised upon an elbow.

"That's him!" Warren whispered. "They're coming in!"

It was a chilling thought. Imagine, a hairy, long-armed giant out there within earshot. There were occasional reports that these things had killed people!

About a minute passed, then there was another whistle like the first. "It's a signal, like an 'all clear,' " Warren whispered. "Everybody stay quiet."

Then it began, a clearly audible rapid-fire chattering, a gibberish that came in spurts punctuated by snorts and an occasional long, drawn-out nasal snarl. Some of it had the ring of monkeys' chatter. Some of it had a barnyard sound. Some of it seemed almost articulate and human. Nearly all of it was loud and raucous, and totally amazing to Alan's ears. There was nothing awkward or distinctly man-made, as he might have supposed from the quality and editing of the reproductions Greg and he had heard at Warren's house. The sounds were clear and fluid—and close by. As Warren, Bill, and Lewis in whispers quietly discussed strategy for the night, Alan became aware that his knees were trembling!

They had made a small hole in the shelter roof by

parting some logs and branches. The plan was for Alan to get up there, push his head and upper torso through it, and photograph the beast. He had second thoughts about the idea now, but as Warren began his "Here Biggie, come on in" patter, he struggled to his feet.

Climbing into the perch was no easy maneuver in the dark interior. It required finding, then wedging one's toes into cracks and openings in the wall, and lifting oneself up through the hole forcibly, using hands, arms, and elbows for leverage. In a nervous state, it was even more difficult. Alan made a good deal of noise fumbling and falling, wrestling with limbs and branches that seemed determined to hold him back.

Like a human periscope Alan finally emerged. As his eyes adjusted to the pale moonlit scene, he could make out a dense cluster of pine and fir where the commotion seemed to originate. The edge of the thicket lay about forty yards uphill, where the hill began to rise steeply. Whatever was hidden there was either ignorant of Alan's outside presence or didn't care, for the utterances continued without any detectable change in tone.

There was a commandingly powerful voice and a slighter, higher-pitched one that seemed responsive to it. It struck Alan that there was some sort of heated, intense, and rather hilarious discussion going on. In a theater it would have been called dramatics. It wasn't particularly frightening, despite his wobbly knees; at the same time, of course, he had a .45-caliber semi-automatic handy and there wasn't any hurry to climb down outside and go rushing up into the trees. There was a slim possibility, obviously, that whatever was up there might decide to show itself and come rushing down to him, in which case all he had to do was drop back down inside through the hole—to hell with any pictures!

Warren, inside the shelter, continued to call out and "talk" to them. His voice was firm, the inflections solicitous. And the creature-things responded to him, it seemed, sometimes with a snort or a high-speed burst of chatter. At one point, the creatures began whining like kids in a kitchen waiting to be fed. Warren suggested that they put food out for them, and after a few minutes he and Lewis emerged from the shelter to set some out. As they appeared, the forest suddenly fell silent.

The offering—a pan of rolled oats, a few apples, and slices of canned meat—was gathered by the men from the cookstove area downhill. As they passed by, walking uphill, they asked Alan the direction of the sounds. He answered them without thinking, out loud, and they exchanged more words as they placed the food where Alan could get a photograph if the things came down to get it. Without realizing it, Alan had revealed himself and his presence outside to the creatures, at least apparently. For as soon as Warren and Lewis were back inside the shelter, a sudden, chillingly angry sound came from the thicket. It began as a growl, only it drew out, building into a loud, vibrating crescendo in which Alan heard what could only be the creature's jowls shaking. It was like a gorilla's display, one can imagine, only the voice was louder than any man's or animal's Alan had ever heard, short of an elephant or perhaps a tiger. He lost his precarious footing, a single toehold in the vertical logjamlike wall inside, and suddenly discovered himself resting on arms and elbows, feet dangling, swinging and kicking rather desperately in the space beneath.

Until he could regain his toehold, he was stuck, caught in the branches in such a way that he could neither pull himself up nor lower himself. For a moment Alan was certain that the thing was going to attack, and he listened for its footsteps coming down the hill. But it didn't come. After a second display like the first, apparently for good measure, the creature then seemed to direct its voice to its companion, and a vigorous and violent-sounding altercation between them ensued. The smaller-voiced creature seemed to be scolding the big one for some reason. I could only imagine that it must have something to do with the food, and Alan's presence there—now altogether obvious, overlooking it. For all the world, from the inflections they sounded like man and wife.

The evening progressed and they did not approach the food or in any way reveal themselves. Alan saw nothing, no suspicious shape or shadow, and no movement. For a long time they continued to jabber off and on, punctuating their thoughts with meaningful-sounding snorts, coughs, and growls. Warren at one point stepped outside the shelter and whistled to them, and was answered in whistles in an exchange that lasted several minutes. To my impression, with the vocalizing that accompanied the whistles, it was not mere mimicry but an attempt at communication.

In the end, after more than an hour, the strangely clear and powerful voices could be heard retreating up the hill and finally faded away in the distance. Several jets had passed high overhead. I wondered if the sound had disturbed the creatures or if they had simply tired of a game? The food remained untouched, and was still there, untouched by any animal, in the morning.

In the morning the men found fresh footprints that seemed to confirm the activity of the night before. The size of them was incredible to Alan, as was the swim-flipper shape; yet, viewing them firsthand, it did seem that they could be flesh and blood impressions rather than something made by a two-by-four. Under the influences of daylight "reality," Alan regressed almost completely to his skeptical self and spent a great deal of time searching for what he now imagined was the "real" evidence: hidden amplifiers, electronic gear, footprints other than their own or those of the creatures, any evidence at all, in short, which would point toward a human connection. He even went through his friends' personal gear, the walls, niches, and crannies of the shelter, the food barrels, and other likely hiding places. He found nothing there, or anywhere, to satisfy his disbelief.

Even more perplexing, on the second night the things came back. And this time it was evident—from a shrill, screechingly imperfect young voice and twelve-inch footprints found later on—that a juvenile was among them.

The men played blindman's buff with them for about

an hour in the moonlit glades and dark forest recesses, with them advancing or retreating according to the men's search and pursuit. At one point, Alan found himself thrashing about in a dense stand of trees—seedlings bunched together—and suddenly had a frightening thought: he'd forgotten to strap on his sidearm. All at once it was very quiet. If a twig had cracked, Alan would have thrown five hundred dollars' worth of camera straight up in the air. He leaped and ran through the thicket, clearing most of the trees it seemed, until he reached an open flat where the others had gathered. As they stood there listening for a few minutes afterward, one of the creatures gamely whistled at them from not far above the very place where Alan had been.

As on the night before, again the creatures' voices finally faded away and there was no discernible "activity" for the remainder of the night. Among footprints and other signs found the following morning was what Alan was certain would become key evidence, regardless how minute. It was a long strand of fine blondish hair that he discovered loosely caught in the boughs of a young, seven-foot-tall evergreen. Around the tree's base, in snow and moist earth, marched a set of nineteen-inch-long footprints, five-toed and fresh from the night before. It appeared that the creature had used the tree for a fulcrum or handhold as it had turned downhill, in the direction of camp. There were no bear or other animal tracks in evidence except the men's own.

A noted University of California zoologist[5] would eventually receive the hair along with other samples. After a year, he would finally return them with his apologies that he could not be more certain of his analyses. He did not believe in Bigfoot, he said. As to the key strand of hair, it was "probably bear."

It was the last week in October. The warm "Indian summer" had passed. The autumnal splash of color had faded, leaving aspen, alder, and other lush but deciduous greenery looking stark and skeletal. In the meadows, broad-leafed skunk cabbage had turned brown and brittle, and it rattled in the wind. Along the creeks and freshets and around the springs, thin layers of ice had formed and crunched loudly underfoot. Winter in the high country was imminent. Soon the access roads would be closed, the area snowbound and isolated.

Larry and Alan had just hiked into camp carrying several camera-trap devices with which Alan had planned to cover the main points of entry and exit there. It was freezing cold and the breeze created an additional chill factor. As quickly as possible, they lit the stove to warm themselves by and had put on water for tea.

Larry was the youngest of the Johnson party. He was a soft-spoken man in his twenties who'd married early, had drifted from job to job on farms and ranches after quitting school to support his family, and only recently had become serious-minded about a career. He was working nights on a poultry ranch, where he hoped to advance to a foreman's slot and have the time and money to resume his education.

After he and Alan had warmed themselves and shared a tin of stew for lunch, they set up a recorder and then began placing the cameras. From the beginning the cold caused problems. Batteries had weakened. Working parts were sluggish. Their fingers quickly numbed, resulting in fumbling and delays. The afternoon soon slipped into early evening and dusk as they struggled to get the last of the devices mounted and operational.

They were still working uphill from the shelter when one of the creatures announced its arrival, or presence, on the scene. It made itself known with a sharp rap of wood against wood, a double rap echoing from a ridgeline above camp.

"Guess who," was Larry's remark.

As they continued their task, sharp, periodic raps continued, sometimes punctuated by a more rapid, insistent-sounding *rap-rap-rap*.

"Sounds like he's trying to tell us something," Larry said. "What do you think, maybe we ought to give this thing up and . . ."

Alan had wanted to complete the trap—there weren't going to be many more opportunities to get pictures of the creatures or make an attempt. But now in the darkening forest there was a hard, emphatic blow, resonant as if made against a hollow log. The creature was coming nearer, it seemed, and it was apparent that it was carrying a club.

"I don't think we ought to keep him waiting," Larry said in earnest. His voice was steady, but his eyes were wide. They tested the equipment once, then left the site, heading downhill toward the cookstove, whose glow could be seen through the trees. Like Larry, Alan didn't want to stand in the fellow's way.

Once inside the shelter, they had every reason to expect vocalization, they heard none—not for a long while. There was, instead, a continuation of the rapping sounds, off and on. Nor did the creature come closer than the approximate area where they had heard the heavy blow against a log, well up on the hill. It seemed he'd positioned himself there for the evening's stay.

Finally they emerged from the shelter, went downhill to the stove, and rekindled the fire. The wind had died, but the temperature had dropped and the cold seemed even more penetrating. They warmed their hands, then took turns stepping out into a clearing with a camera. "Come on fella, come on down. See, we only want to take your picture. See the camera, it won't hurt you. This is how it's done. Nothing to it. Now come on and let's be friends."

As long as the men remained outside, the woods uphill remained silent. But just as soon as they would retire to the shelter, the rapping would begin, again with no vocalization.

They tried the "retiring" routine several more times before giving up hope for some interesting action. Larry finally buried himself under a pile of old sleeping bags, used usually for padding underneath, and within a short time had begun to snore. A down bag was warm and snug enough for Alan's own comfort, but he found that he couldn't sleep. For every *rap-rap* outside, it seemed, there was some new thought or question.

About a half-hour had passed when suddenly there was a change in the performance uphill. Alan shook Larry, urging him to wake up and listen.

It began with six or seven beats in succession, sharp, resounding smacks, then one, two, and three in what seemed to be an alternating rhythmic sequence. Then there was a lapse and what sounded like someone with a deep, resonant, nasal voice mumbling incoherently. The mumbling rose in pitch, opening out into a series of sonorous, almost singsong, "umm-oh/oh-ahhs." It had a primitive texture. It was like a chant Alan had once heard in a Japanese monastery, something that welled out of the gut and droned on and on. All the loneliness, or was it oneness, in the world seemed wrapped up in the strange song. Alan was moved by it, by its simplicity and the mood or feeling it conveyed. It was at once mournful and melancholy, wanting and sad—not unlike a dirge, perhaps, yet in its force it also conveyed a feeling that there was nothing to be done but listen and carry on. Finally it trailed off in a low hum and ended abruptly in a deep cough. The measured, rhythmic beating followed, then a series of vigorous fast beats, and finally silence.

Larry said that he recognized the voice as that of one they called the Old Man. They'd seen his track on occasion. He left prints two feet long. He was the only creature that had ever screamed at the men, and that had only happened once, when they'd apparently surprised him in close quarters and had followed his trail in pursuit.

Larry was affected much as Alan had been. They had both listened in silence. They had both been moved. What was wrong, they wondered. Was it ill? Had one of them died? Had it been abandoned by the others with winter's approach? What had become of the terrible, sometimes funny chatter and brawling sounds?

Through the night the song was repeated every so often, without much variation if any, it seemed. Alan became convinced that the creature was alone, that it was addressing them, as opposed to the wilderness around, with its soulful message. Alan still could not

sleep. Or if he did, it was fitfully, and he awakened
instantly to the sound, to listen and wonder all the
more.

With dawn they arose and left the shelter, and Alan
went to check the cameras. He knew that none had
been tripped. He had a feeling that none ever would
be tripped by the creatures. What he found was that
none would have tripped save the last one installed.
Each was frozen tight. They searched the hill and found
no sign of their visitor or his log instrument. The
ground everywhere was frozen and unyielding. The pine
mat revealed no trace.

Back at the shelter, Alan thought to check out the
tape recorder. It too had felt the cold's bite. The song
was lost. What remained was the memory.

It was several nights later, on another trip, that
Warren and Alan would hear the creature a final time.
It had made a single pass, rapping its way along the
ridgeline above camp with the sounds trailing off the far
side below. The Old Man's track has not been found
and he has not been heard from since.

Nor were any of the others heard from, although
their footprints were occationally found, until two years
later, in October 1974. It seemed as if with the close of
the 1972 season, the family had moved off, abandoning
the lush mountain area. Bears moved in and the bees
hummed, but for everyone involved, the creatures'
absence was a great disappointment. Between Warren,
Lewis, Larry, Bill McDowell, Ron Moorehead, a few
family members and close friends, and Alan Berry
himself—now a somewhat chastened skeptic—many
weeks were spent on the mountain waiting for the creatures' return. The dialogue had only begun; it didn't
seem fair that it might be finished.

NOTES

1. The Society for the Investigation of the Unexplained, Columbia, N.J. 07832. Johnson had attempted to enlist the aid of the late Ivan T. Sanderson, zoologist, prominent society member, and author of *Abominable Snowmen: Legend Come to Life*.

2. The Bigfoot Information Center, P.O. Box 632, The Dalles, Ore. 97058. The center operates as a clearing house for Bigfoot reports. A "Board of Examiners," of which Alan Berry is a member, was recently appointed to assist in investigations. The center publishes a monthly newsletter, *Bigfoot News*. Its geographical area of concern is primarily northern California, Oregon, Washington, and British Columbia.

3. At the time, Peter Byrne had remarked, "If Johnson's findings are true, they're absolutely extraordinary."

4. Greg Lyon, Associated Press award-winner for a series of articles first exposing huckster Glen Turner's Koscot cosmetics enterprises as a fraudulent "pyramid" promotional scheme, now reporting for the *National Enquirer*.

5. Dr. Seth Benson, Professor Emeritus of Zoology, now retired.

3

Pursuers or the Pursued?

The Johnson case was unusual enough, even in the annals of Bigfoot investigations, without any added twist of the bizarre. But Alan Berry wasn't writing the script, nor, he is convinced, were the others.

One of the first clues that there might be something truly extraordinary about the Sierra Bigfoot people—something other than what their voices, footprints, and an occasional strand of hair suggested—was their uncanny ability to avoid being seen or photographed. Direct Bigfoot encounters are rare and usually accidental, but they frequently involve a sighting. Here was a case where there were repeated, rather lengthy encounters, with not one but several of the creatures, with at least two, and often more, witnesses present. Yet with the exception of Lewis' account, there had been no sightings except for fleeting shapes, shadows, a "movement" as Larry had said, and "blobs floating" among the trees, as Warren would describe one moment. The men had tried various ploys. They'd tried hiding in a hollow stump, under a tarpaulin on the ground, and in the branches on the shelter roof, and had been met with eerie silence. They'd tried springing from the shelter's door at the sound of the creatures' footsteps nearby outside, to see nothing and hear nothing. They'd tried camera traps and had found them torn down. As much as they wanted "proof" of the creatures to satisfy an outsider's curiosity, their first interest was in obtaining some kind of tangible proof for themselves. The mutual desire was nearly obsessive by the time Alan arrived on the scene. There were periodic debates on whether to attempt shooting one of the creatures. If one could be brought down, the event would make history. But what if the thing was more human than animal— would they have committed murder? What about the betrayal of their outward trust and show of friendliness —would the other creatures turn violent? In addition, there was a practical problem: rarely was there ever a visible target, despite the closeness of the voices and footsteps. There were times when it almost seemed as if the creatures could make themselves invisible, and disappear in a split second. It wasn't a thought that any of the men warmed to or liked to discuss, yet, inexorably, it would surface: were there spiritual or other unknown forces at play?

Two persons gifted with extrasensory perception (ESP) inadvertently became involved peripherally with the case. Both parties, whose identities will not be revealed, seemed to predict rather accurately important changes that would occur on the mountain. Neither of them, it should be said, had any specific knowledge of the camp, the Sierra region, Bigfoot stories per se, or members of the Johnson party; yet both, it seems, were able in varying degrees to "see" the camp, the area, the men, and even the creatures, and remark about events that either were taking place or would take place at some time in the future.

One of the ESP persons was introduced to Alan shortly after he had witnessed his first Bigfoot activity in camp; he offered the following: The creature family was nomadic, usually moved through a broad area of the middle and southern Sierras from season to season, but had developed an attachment, partly emotional and partly out of curiosity, for the camp and its men. The leader, a male who "could be less but no more than" twelve feet tall, was born and reared in southern Oregon and was "close to" eighty years old; he had a human-like face, was "very intelligent," was thin for his height, weighing about six hundred pounds, and he had "blond or gray" hair due to his age. The rest of the "family"—including two adult males, two adult females, a seven-year-old "boy of the woods" who was big for his age, and a 160-pound, six-foot-tall, three-year-old female "baby"—all had "darker" hair.

As of the night on which Larry Johnson and Alan had listened to the Old Man's incantations, according to the ESP person the elder male's authority had been challenged by a younger male, and part of the family had moved a few miles southward to a lower elevation. "The Big One has only two with him now, one male and one female," the person said. The argument, it seems, had had something to do with the "Big One's" health and ability to keep up with the younger members of the clan. It was doubtful that he would live another full season. Instinctively he was drawn to the north and east, to a harsher climate where he was certain to perish without the others' support. He'd wanted them to go with him. When the younger leader objected and insisted that the group move southward, the Old Man had grown adamant and had stayed behind. If he remained stubborn, the person said, the companion pair would leave him and rejoin the others. The delay and question was, had he reached his dying time? The pair would remain with him only until it was apparent that he'd arrived at some decision. "When he reaches a decision, they all will be together again. But they must move soon. Food is now a problem, and they are worried about people invading their other areas. . . ."

If the ESP person's description of the creatures and the Old Man's plight was nothing more than a sensi-

tive imagination building on given facts, it remains a
wonder that a few days afterward, on the final hike into
camp, the creatures *were* encountered at a lower elevation south of camp. The location was near the base of a
trail leading to the higher elevations, an area cited in
specific detail by the person. The creatures had whistled,
and there was some chatter, and the men had hiked on
into camp assuming that it was a greeting party of some
sort and that it would return and they'd all be in the
area waiting for them. Instead, the men had simply
heard the periodic rapping coming from a ridge above
camp as one, it seemed, slowly made its way downward,
headed south.

It was not until the following March that the ESP-
gifted person would offer anything further about the
creatures, and it would be a final submission. The family at the time was situated near a national park about a
hundred miles south of camp, the person indicated. They
would be returning to the region of the camp in mid-
June. However, it would be "useless" to attempt to re-
establish contact. The old male was still with the group,
but a younger one had assumed leadership and was in
control. He was opposed to any further communication
with the humans and would see that they were avoided.
There was a slim chance, it seemed, that a juvenile, "the
boy of the woods" who'd become somewhat of a maverick, would come into camp, but there would be little
if any activity other than that. In addition, the person
said, a research project proposal that Alan had written
to obtain technical assistance and funds for the summer,
would be to no avail. "The letters will go to the wrong
people. Private letters should be sent to people who like
him [Bigfoot]."

The research proposal, along with an account of the
Sierra Bigfoot phenomena, nevertheless went out to a
number of foundations and institutions, and plans were
roughed out for a summer expedition. There followed a
long wait and no replies—not even form-letter acknowl-
edgments of receipt. But this did not daunt anyone. By
the second week in June, an expedition that would begin

with two, Warren and Alan, supported by two mules packing food and equipment, was climbing the initial 2,400 vertical feet of trail.

They would dip into their own finances and time. Between Warren and his crew, Alan, his brother Bob, and Fred Benton,[1] many weeks were spent in and about the onetime Basque sheep camp through the 1973 and 1974 seasons, searching, hoping and hunting for the elusive Bigfoot band. As the ESP person had predicted, their efforts were to little avail. There were occasional signs that the creatures were in the general area, but they were neither talking nor making themselves known. During one night in June 1973, a single creature was heard as it walked rather noisily through camp; the following morning they made casts of its fourteen-inch-long footprint on a soft embankment where it had crossed a creek. Was this the maverick "boy of the woods"? There was no other activity—except a total of eleven different black bears that discovered the expedition's food stores during one two-week period—until the following September, when two sets of larger footprints were found. During the 1974 season there was no sign of the creatures at all, until mid-August.

Among other things, in the interim Alan continued soliciting outside help and scientific interest in the case. At first he wasn't concerned with researchers whose names were already associated with the phenomenon, such as Peter Byrne; he was looking for authority which was basically uninformed, which he felt would be more impartial and objective.

The creatures' vocalizations he had taped were offered to a number of universities, institutions, and individual specialists in the mechanics of sound. One primate behaviorist[2] with impeccable credentials asserted that the sounds were definitely primate, but expressed skepticism that they were of a primate order lower than man—because primates lower than man can't, or don't, whistle. A University of California linguist[3] listened to a portion of the sounds played backward, and cautiously speculated that they must be a Chinese dialect, filtered, scrambled, and reconstituted somehow. A University of Connecticut linguist[4] known for his studies of primate vocalization thought that a former student of his was "pulling his leg"; the sounds were obviously phony, it seemed, a simple matter of a few hours' work on a human voice with a tape splicer and a band-pass filtering machine.

Few of the specialists approached seemed able to think beyond a presumption of hoax. None offered more than what seemed to be a reluctant cursory analysis. So, eventually, Alan privately retained an acoustics laboratory, Syntonic Research, Inc., of New York, which had worked with animal sounds, had exposed animal-sound hoaxes, and had a growing reputation in the commercial field of sound. After expressing initial skepticism, the company, whose time few individual investigators could afford, gave some of its valuable time gratuitously and even tried to enlist outside scientific interest in the New York area. Its conclusions were that the vocalizations had occurred at the time of the original recording, were spontaneous, and were, given mike-to-source distances of one hundred feet or more, too powerful to have been human-made. Its recommendation was that Alan try to find a reputable university-based sound lab that would tackle the tapes "in the interests of science" on a gratuitous basis, and provide a more complete analysis. (See Appendix B.)

The significance of Syntonic's report, however incomplete the analysis, seemed clear: the sounds were not a playback of something orchestrated by man, nor were they the result of some clever electronic manipulation of tapes, which had been the presumption of nearly every expert Alan had previously approached.

One of the original tapes subsequently went to the Naval Weapons Center at China Lake, California, then chimpanzee expert Jane Goodall was approached, and the Primate Research Center at Stanford University. The Naval Weapons Center held the tape for six months and returned it with no comment. Jane Goodall said the Bigfoot subject was fascinating and wished us all good luck. The Primate Research Center said it was

sorry but there was no one available who was competent and interested in examining the sounds.

A. F. Bischoff of San Jose, a signal analyst employed
by a major U.S. electronics corporation, while working
privately under the auspices of that corporation, would
eventually volunteer to do a more comprehensive study
of the tapes and sounds. His report may be found in
Appendix B.

While one of the ESP-gifted persons had foretold the
creatures' retreat from human contact, the other had
predicted, about two months in advance, a resumption
of Bigfoot activity about camp which was to occur
late in the 1974 season. It would be important for
someone to be on hand, the source said, for new knowledge of the creatures would be "revealed."

What was this supposed to mean? Beginning on the
second weekend of August 1974 there was a form of
unusual activity at camp and creature footprints were
found. Warren, Lewis, Larry, and another of Warren's
sons, ten-year-old David, were in camp. As on nearly
every night there, some time was spent after dinner and
before retiring talking quietly around the cookstove. On
this evening, however, there was little talk, and what
there was seemed to come in hushed, self-conscious
tones. There was a mutual awareness, a sense of an
outside presence, it seemed, which in the past had
usually signaled Bigfoot activity. Only there was apprehension now, not mere expectancy. Warren, Lewis,
and Larry had exchanged wondering glances but otherwise, because of David, had tried to conceal their feelings. David, who had been to the camp a few times before but never when there was any creature activity,
first began to shake, then suddenly burst into tears.

He was sitting on a log beside his father. Ashamedly,
he buried his face in his hands. "Daddy, I'm scared!" he
said. "I'm scared inside!"

Warren put his arms around the boy and tried to
reassure him that there was nothing to be frightened
about "But I could sense what he was feeling because
I was feeling the same thing myself," he said. "It was

a clammy feeling, there was a tension in the air. Larry and Lewis felt it too. . . ."

Nothing else unusual happened that night, however. A deer that had been frequenting the camp even approached, looking for a handout. They'd named her Molly. David had quickly recovered. The feelings of apprehension had passed.

By the boy's bedtime the following night, the incident had been nearly forgotten. Nothing unusual had happened during the day, and they'd spent a relaxed evening. Molly had reconnoitered the camp once again, and they'd put out salt for her. There'd been little reference to the creatures. Nothing had been seen or heard to indicate they were anywhere in the vicinity—except for the period of strange, ominous feelings the night before.

Warren was inside the shelter with David, helping him arrange his sleeping bag and get settled for the night, when suddenly one of the others shouted from down at the cookstove, "Hey, did you guys just shine a flashlight this way?"

Light inside the shelter, whose walls were made of thick logs and lesser material and were, in places, two feet thick, could barely be seen outside—only through a thin crack here and there. Warren's muffled voice came back that, no, he hadn't shone his flashlight outside.

"Well, there's something funny going on," Lewis shouted back, "because there was a bright flash from up there that just lit up the whole area."

As both Warren and his son emerged from the shelter, there was another "flash." "I was looking right at it," Warren said. "It was like a strobe light, it lit up the whole camp scene."

He said it seemed to have come from about fifteen feet above ground about thirty feet away, in the trees. "David was right behind me and saw the same thing except that we are in disagreement about one of the details. To me it seemed like the light source or whatever was round and ball-like, maybe two to three feet in diameter, and it had a bluish cast and a white band around it. David describes it the same way, only he remembers it as being white with a bluish band around it —just the opposite."

There was no sound associated with it, he said. Warren also claimed that, even though the flash was brilliant, it was not blinding and did not seem to affect his night vision.

As he and his son started downhill toward Lewis and Larry, there was a third flash, and this one seemed to give off a diffuse greenish light that briefly illuminated an area of about one hundred feet in diameter beneath the taller trees. It had "exploded" off to one side, Warren said, but in a different location from the first one they'd seen.

They joined Larry and Lewis in a clearing halfway between the shelter and the cookstove, and as the party stood there watching in amazement, more flashes went off in the surrounding trees. Warren began timing them with his wristwatch, which showed that it was 10:45 P.M. For the next fifteen minutes or so, it seemed that the mysteriously silent light explosions were occurring at two-minute intervals.

"At first we thought it might be static electricity," he said, "because we didn't move very much while we watched. Mostly, we just stood still. But when we began to move around, we found out that the more we moved, the faster the flashes came. I walked up to the shelter and back, and it seemed like every six to eight feet a light would explode somewhere in the trees overhead. It was so quick you couldn't always tell where it was coming from. Aside from what David and I saw, there were only a couple of times that anybody actually got a look at the source."

In one experiment he and Lewis walked to a clearing uphill, leaving Larry and David at the shelter to watch the effects. "We wanted to see if the lights would follow us," Warren said. And the lights did follow them, it seems, exploding every so often in different locations overhead. Larry saw one of them just as it went off. The light seemed to come from something bright about the size of a basketball, he said.

The static electricity theory seemed to be the right answer when they found that by shuffling their feet on the pine mat, they could "cause" the flashes to occur. Yet the weather conditions didn't support the theory: there was no wind, the skies were clear, the humidity seemed normal, and it was a cool 56 degrees. At one point they heard a high-pitched whining noise that began near where they were standing and seemed to trail off at a distance, and they began to wonder about this.

"There was nothing frightening about it," Warren recalled. "Even David will tell you—he was as calm as any of us. But it was a curious thing. What it reminded you of was like someone taking pictures all over the place, using a flash attachment . . . only we had no feeling that we were actually being watched or threatened in any way."

The light effects tapered off in frequency and finally ceased about midnight, and everyone went to bed. But about 3:15 A.M., Warren said, he was awakened by a mouse scampering about near his head. "As I listened," Warren said, "the little guy suddenly decided to use my head for a springboard to jump on my pack, which was leaning up against the wall. He made just one mistake, and that was sitting still for a moment where he landed. I nailed him with the palm of my hand and must have knocked him clear across the shelter. What happened, though, was that just as I hit him, almost simultaneously, a light flashed *inside* the shelter, right by the door. Larry and Lewis were both immediately awakened by it, it was so intense. Then, in rapid succession, maybe a second or two apart, there were five or six more—all intensely bright, greenish flashes. Then they stopped and we saw nothing more. We shined our flashlights around everywhere but couldn't find anything, and there was no sound, nothing at all. . . ."

Beginning at dusk the following night, there was more of the strange light activity in a pattern similar to the preceding evening's flurry of flashes. Again there were few clues to its origin or cause, except for the possibility of some unknown atmospheric condition. It seemed as if it were a natural phenomenon, yet in some ways it seemed manifestly controlled: *some* times the men could shuffle their feet and cause it to occur, but at other times they couldn't—it would be off blipping by itself in the trees elsewhere. And what of the odd, high-pitched tuning-fork sound they'd heard?

There was yet another factor that was difficult to ignore: in their daytime hikes, the region surrounding the camp seemed strangely quiet, totally devoid of all bird and animal noise. Molly, the deer that appeared in the evenings, seemed to be the only creature around, aside from themselves.

On the fourth day, Warren and David hiked out and returned home. Lewis and Larry stayed on. "Lewis didn't want to stay but Larry did," Warren said, "and Lewis finally agreed. It was beginning to get to all of us, I think, but Lewis in particular. He was getting jumpy."

That evening the light activity began just as the sun was setting behind a ridgeline to the west, while there was still plenty of daylight. However, this time it seemed to concentrate more on the men, flashing directly over their heads. And as darkness fell it became apparent that the lights were much more intense than previously. "They followed us around," Larry said. "Just to see what would happen, Hick [Larry's nickname for Lewis] and I walked over into the clearing beyond the spring, and they were with us all the way. I looked up once just as one went off and it was like looking into a cone. And they really lighted up the area. You know the boulder pile down across the creek? It was a couple of hundred feet from where we stopped, and you could see it just like daylight every time one went off."

The following morning, in the same open area, a slope covered with grass, deep scrub brush, and patches of sandy, decomposing granite, they discovered a set of Bigfoot prints. It appeared as if the creature had been running, had come down off the slope, turned toward the camp, and stopped next to spring, where there were thick, ten-foot-high clumps of mountain alder, and the soil was boggy. From the best print, they saw that the creature's foot was about twenty inches long. In shape and proportions, the print was not unlike all the others that had been found in and around camp. Yet several things puzzled the men.

One was the mysterious way the track ended. The creature had come downhill from an area of boulders and high brush, so they were not surprised when they could backtrack it no farther than the edge of the brush. But it did seem that there should be some indication of where the creature went beyond the last print, whose direction was toward the spring. This ground was soft and mushy there, and anything heavy should have left additional impressions—even allowing for the creature's apparent speed and gigantic step. Where had it gone?

Another concern was the creature's apparent haste. The depth of the impressions, skid marks, and the great stride—twelve feet on the downhill side to eight feet in the turn—all suggested that the creature was in a hurry and running hard. What had caused it to run?

The most puzzling piece of all the evidence, however, was what Larry discovered at the spring: bloodstains in the grass and on the ground, and a thumb-sized piece of torn and bloody flesh that resembled lung tissue. He and Lewis had heard distant gunfire that morning. Had one of the creatures been shot? Were they the flesh and blood of some other animal that had been killed, a portion of which had been brought to the spring? Was there, in fact, any relationship between the footprints and the flesh? What of the strange light activity, did it somehow tie in?

In the wake of the light activity, the bloody finds were disturbing enough to prompt the men to hurriedly close down camp and backpack out of the area. They were halfway home, driving along the highway, still discussing the possible meaning of their discoveries, before it occurred to either of them that they should have saved the piece of flesh to have it analyzed and identified. They'd left it where they found it, near the spring. By the time the next party arrived in camp a few days later, both the torn piece of flesh and the bloodstains were gone; only the footprints remained.

While the flashing lights may have resulted from an unusual but natural atmospheric condition, the men would experience yet another type of phenomenon that would leave them wondering about the second psychic's prediction. As with the lights, it too would invade the confines of their shelter and have an unsettling effect on the men's sense of security there. It was a sound effect, a staccato ticking that resembled the noise produced by a Geiger counter, a telegraph key, canvas being ripped.[5]

It began on a night when Bill McDowell and Ron Moorehead were staying in camp, about three weeks after the last of the light activity. They'd ridden into camp on horseback, arriving late in the afternoon. The two men unpacked, opened camp, turned the animals loose in the corral, prepared an evening's meal at the stove, and retired to bed in the shelter.

"I was just about asleep," Bill said, "when I heard this sound like canvas ripping—a blur almost—and it seemed like it was coming from somewhere inside the shelter. I said, 'Hey, did you hear that?' Ron answered, 'Yeah, where's it coming from?' I sat up in my bag so I could try to pinpoint the sound. It sounded like it was coming right out of the wall about five feet above where Ron was on the other side of the shelter.

"Well, Ron sat up too, and we flashed our lights around and couldn't see anything, and the noise stopped. But Ron said he was certain that the noise had come from the wall over *my* head. So we got up and changed places, then turned our flashlights off. And, sure enough, we heard the sound again. Only now it seemed to me that the sound really was coming from over Ron's head, where I'd been just a minute before, and I said, 'Hey, you were right, it's coming from over there where you are.' He said, 'No, it can't be. I heard it perfectly. It came from over your head, right where you said it was in the first place, when I was over there and you were over here. . . .' "

Again they beamed their flashlights around the shelter, then resumed their original positions. Whenever their lights were turned on, the sounds stopped, at least at first. As they continued to listen, the noise seemed to fade in and fade out, and also move about inside the shelter. Sometimes it was less like canvas ripping and more like the tapping of a telegraph key, slower and more emphatic. Sometimes it grew quite loud. After about an hour, it would continue despite the shining of flashlights and any talk or discussion.

"I'd been listening to the thing for quite a while and it sounded like it was across on the other side of the shelter, when all of a sudden it was clicking right in front of my nose," Ron recalled. "I said, 'Hey, what the heck is going on here?' I grabbed my flashlight and shined it right in front of my face, but there wasn't anything there. I tried feeling around the space where it was coming from, but couldn't feel anything. But we could both hear it, and this time we agreed where it was, right there in front of my eyes. Only there was nothing there, just space. . . ."

"Ron was getting a little frantic," Bill said. "It wasn't like a buzzing insect or that we were imagining things, there was something there . . . we got some of the sounds on tape."

At one point the clicking ceased, and they heard "heavy footsteps crunching around on the pine mat" outside the shelter. Something "rustled" a plastic tarpaulin that lined the shelter's roof and was exposed in places outside. "We could hear it moving the brush back and forth and touching the plastic," Bill recalled. He said they got up and went outside, but saw and heard nothing unusual. The horses downhill at the small makeshift corral showed no reaction, it seemed. They'd remained quiet throughout the entire episode.

As with Bigfoot activity in the past, and as it had been with the weird flashing lights, the metallic tapping, clicking, or whatever eventually ceased, and the men finally fell asleep.

On succeeding nights, however, it would return, and off and on they would again hear the sounds of heavy footfalls outside, and the rustling of brush and plastic on the shelter's roof. They were joined by Lewis and Warren, who also experienced the strange effects. The heavy footsteps had to be "Biggie" and his kind skulking about, they all agreed, only there was no vocalization, thumping, whistles, or even the sound of breathing when the creature was obviously close by, within a few feet outside the shelter. And when Warren or one of the others would suddenly jump outside through the door in an effort to see the thing, there would not even be sounds of it moving away. It was as if there were nothing there, nothing to be seen, anyway.

As in the case of the lights, except for a single instance where the sounds of wood being jarred made it seem "like the thing was coming through the wall," the men experienced little fright or apprehension with either the tapping noises or the footfalls and rustling outside. "We didn't rush for our guns," Ron later said. "We'd get up and shine our lights around outside, or we'd sit up in our bags listening and talking while the noise went on, just trying to figure out what was causing it and what was going on."

As with the lights, they tried experiments. "One time," Bill recalled, "Ron called out when we heard footsteps outside, 'Hey Biggie, is that you out there?' And there was suddenly a rapid ticking inside, like in response—it was like a retort."

The men's primary feeling, it seemed, was frustration, ". . . frustration over hearing the sound only two feet away from you and not being able to see anything."

Strange metallic clicking, heavy footfalls heard that left no physical evidence of their maker (no footprints ever were found after such activity around the shelter), flashing lights, a trace of violence at the spring, and the track of a creature on the run—what did it all mean? Was it all related? Was any of it related? Was there some "perfectly natural" explanation?

The second psychic person had predicted revelations. However, what the Johnson party seemed to have experienced during these weeks was a deepening of the Bigfoot mystery, an unexpected, disheartening turn of events. The men had believed, and still wanted to believe, that the creatures were biological, flesh-and-blood beings. The current "activity" and evidence, if it were related to Bigfoot, had left them wanting.

Deer-hunting season opened in late September. As had been the custom in the past, several of the men would be in camp for the opening weekend. As had also been the custom, they would try to arrive there on the preceding Friday night, so they could be up early and out on the mountainside hunting with Saturday's dawn. This year, however, Bill McDowell and Ron Moorehead (on his first deer hunt) rode in on horseback a day early, on Thursday night, in vague hopes that there might be some creature activity before the shooting began. For the first time in nearly two years, their hopes would be realized.

The first sign was a blatantly conspicuous, eighteen-inch-long fresh footprint in the middle of the trail, about two hours' ride from camp. It seemed as if the creature had crossed the trail, moving upward through the manzanita and brush, just ahead of them.

They arrived in camp at dusk, unpacked, put the horses in the corral, and quickly set about preparing a meal at the cookstove. The shelter did not appear to have been tampered with in their absence and everything about camp seemed normal, except for their mutual delight at having found the footprint earlier and a sense of expectancy.

They did not have long to wait. Even before the fire had been kindled in the stove, there were the familiar sounds of footfalls and cracking branches out among the trees, now growing dark with the closing nightfall. Then a spate of jabbering and a whooplike call. They could not mask their excitement: it really *was* the creatures, it was *them,* and they'd really come back! And they'd made their presence known while the men were still outside the shelter in the open, almost as they'd arrived. To Ron it was going to be "a great night." Bill, more reflective, recalled, "With us outside like that, I just hoped they were feeling friendly." They dug into their packs for their tape recorders and sat down on logs by the stove to listen.

The creatures, what seemed to be a pair of them, approached from a heavily forested area across a small creek below camp. They came up into the trees about

150 feet away, it seemed, near the camp latrine, where they proceeded to jabber excitedly like long-lost friends at a reunion.

For a while, neither Ron nor Bill said anything except in whispers between themselves. But what seemed to be the more vocal of the creatures began whooping —an "oo-oo" that rose and slipped into a high falsetto before breaking off—as if it were calling out to them. Ron falteringly attempted a whoop in return. The creature responded, it seemed, with a guttural giggling sound, as if it was greatly amused, and whooped again. And soon there was an exchange going, broken up only by the men's soft-spoken asides and the creatures' chattering, chortling, and what seemed to be a great deal of fun-making—as if they were sharing an endless private joke. Every so often there would be the whack of wood against wood, a slap, as if they were hitting each other or themselves, and at one point, one of them took the lid of a toilet seat mounted over the latrine and banged it several times. This immediately resulted in a fresh spate of gleeful-sounding whoops, chortling, and chatter, to which Ron responded by showing his own amusement, attempting to imitate a few of the more articulate sounds.

The creatures eventually moved back downhill and across the creek to a more open area, behind an outcropping of granite boulders. They continued the performance from there until Ron turned on his flashlight so he could see to turn over the cassette cartridge in his tape recorder. The light momentarily flashed out into the trees in the direction of the creek. As if he'd turned a switch off, the creatures fell silent and apparently left the area.

The following night, Lewis, Larry, and Warren arrived in camp. But there was no repeat of the creature activity. On Saturday the men hunted, and a deer was hung beside the shelter. On Sunday morning, several faint Bigfoot prints were found on the ground beneath it, though there was no evidence that the carcass had been touched or molested.

That afternoon the men hunted again and another deer was hung outside the shelter. And that evening, as on the evening Ron and Bill had arrived, the creatures revealed their presence briefly, for what now seems to have been a final time.

The men had finished supper and were sitting around the stove when several whoops were heard from across the creek, in the area of the granite rock outcropping. Unlike the calls and chatter Ron and Bill had heard three nights earlier, however, these sounds did not seem jocular or very friendly; they were pained expressions, more of an angry outcry, it seemed. It affected Lewis almost immediately. After a few minutes, he stood up suddenly and grabbed his rifle from where it leaned against a tree. Saying to the others that he was going to "do something" and "find out once and for all," he walked off downhill, toward the creek.

As soon as Lewis moved, the sounds ceased. Warren then got up, told him to take it easy, and tried to stop him. Lewis had not gone far, but when he returned, he seemed angry and upset. He talked, as another member of the party had a few seasons before, about finding another place to hunt. He'd had enough, he said. It was getting so he couldn't get any sleep when he was on the mountain. Whatever the creatures were, whatever the lights and other strange occurrences meant, it was all getting on his nerves. He just wanted *them* to leave him alone.

They would leave him alone. As it happened, after his outburst there was no more creature activity of any kind, then or afterward, up to the time of this writing. Nor would there be any other unusual phenomena for the remainder of the 1974 season and the entire 1975 season. The camp was monitored. Some of the men would spend a few nights there every other week or so. But the camp with its trees, creek, and spring seemed to have reverted to its natural state, the same pristine setting that Warren, his family, and his friends had enjoyed and become accustomed to for nearly twenty years prior to the creatures' arrival.

There was one further incident, but it happened far from the High Sierra camp in a foothill pasture owned by one of the men.

A sick heifer had been reported in a creek bottom there. The man had gone to investigate. It was several minutes' walk from where he parked his vehicle. As he began the short walk he became aware of a "ticking" to one side and a little behind him. Whenever he'd stop, it would stop. When he'd move on, the tick would begin again and move along with him, always, it seemed, about two feet off the ground and about ten feet away.

It followed him to the site where the heifer was found, dead of a disease, then followed him again part of the way back, always at about the same distance and a little behind. He said that he knew it had to be an insect of some kind, because there wasn't any other rational explanation. Yet he'd felt chills all the way, he said. "I *knew* that sound the minute I heard it, but I just couldn't believe that's what it was."

NOTES

1. Fred Benton, poet-author of "Looking Across: A Tribute to Bigfoot," *Mountain Gazette,* July 1975.
2. Dr. William Mason, Yerkes Regional Primate Center, University of California at Davis.
3. Jarvis Bastion, University of California at Davis.
4. Dr. Philip Lieberman, University of Connecticut.
5. At the time of this writing, tapes of these sounds are being analyzed.

4

Terror in a Mountain Resort

Thomas E. Smith of Portland, Oregon, writes, "In late June of 1972, a friend and I went fishing in the Cascades at the base of Mt. Jefferson. I don't know the name of the lake or if it has one. I do know that we had been able to reach it only after descending a very steep, boulder-strewn cliff for perhaps a thousand feet.

"As we sat in our two-man rubber raft on the lake, enjoying the great fishing, my friend mentioned something about having visitors, a couple of 'guys' standing near our packs on shore. As we rowed closer, my friend declared, 'Those are apes!' My back was to them as I rowed.

"I turned to see them. They weren't huge. The largest was perhaps six foot. The other was maybe four feet tall and a darker color, almost a dark brown. We thought them perhaps a female and her offspring. They didn't run. They watched us as we watched them. Only when we started to drift closer did they seem nervous and begin to move about. They were graceful and not at all fierce-looking. Finally, they just walked away toward the boulders and we lost sight of them about halfway up the cliff.

"I am not a very good artist but here is the nearest I could come to putting the Bigfoot on paper. It seems the head was longer than in my drawing and the mouth seems wrong. I may have been trying to emphasize the gentleness I saw in the creature." (See illustration.)

Gentleness. Curiosity. Intelligence. Lack of aggression. These and other human qualities have made some Bigfoot witnesses unable to fire although the creature is lined up in their gunsights. . . .

Like Richard Brown of The Dalles, Oregon, in June 1971:

> Brown, a junior-high-school teacher and his wife were returning from a church choir practice. As they drove into their home on the outskirts of The Dalles, the headlights of their car caught a huge creature standing under a tree in a nearby field.
>
> Brown ran into his mobile home for his rifle, which was equipped with a high-powered telescope. In the telescope sight the huge creature made a perfect target. As Brown started to squeeze the trigger, he froze. In the dim light, the monster appeared to be human. As he studied the creature, it turned and walked away.

Bob Watt
Hood River, Oregon, *News*
June 26, 1975

Like explorer Robert Morgan of the American Yeti Expedition in the winter of 1957:

> The heavy crunch of dry, trampled brush. The hunter's trained ear followed the crackling leaves. Through the rifle sight, he tracked whatever was there as it smashed straight through the brambly thicket. In the same instant, eye and animal reached the clearing and stopped—cold.

The two stood staring at each other. Seconds slowed to eons, as each kept a steady eye on the presumed intruder—the other.

Curiosity stayed the animal. Shock stayed the hunter. Too paralyzed to act, he felt his high-powered rifle shrink to a toy.

The animal made no effort to move, no indication of advance. The creature's look was clear, cool, and intelligent. It was not the stare of a wild animal. It was an almost human expression of surprised interest. A mirror of the hunter himself.

Penelope McPhee
"Man Against Myth: The Search for Bigfoot"
The Spokesman-Review Sunday Magazine
September 8, 1974

There appears to be one exception to Bigfoot's reported normally benign nature. He hates dogs. The following are excerpts from just a few documented cases over the years revealing this more hostile facet of the creature's disposition.

October 1947:

Ron Olson, of Eugene, Oregon, a full-time Sasquatch investigator, has a clipping quoting Glenn Payne of Sedalia, Missouri, about a hunt for a creature that had been killing sheep and goats. He said that he saw by the car lights a giant, hairy, man-shaped thing running ahead of his hounds. Later it killed some of the dogs, frightening off the others, and when the men returned to their Jeep they found it overturned.

John Green
The Sasquatch File

October 1958:

NEW BLUFF CREEK MYSTERY
PUZZLES INDIAN:
4 DOGS FOUND RIPPED TO PIECES
The Humboldt Times, Oct. 19, 1958
An Indian who works near the Humboldt-Del Norte County line believes he may have discovered

signs of a Bigfoot temper fit, a Eureka man told
The Humboldt Times yesterday. Harold C. Goodwin, 66, said Curtis Mitchell, an Indian who works
for him, discovered the mutilated bodies of four
dogs last Sunday evening. "He told me they looked
like they'd been ripped apart," Goodwin said. . . .
The Indian told Goodwin that all of the dogs had
been torn apart and one of them had apparently
been slammed against a tree.

                                              Roger Patterson
      Do Abominable Snowmen of America Really Exist?

Early 1960s:

Jay Roland, Willow Creek, tells of finding Bigfoot tracks near his campfire at night after two
hounds had been killed by something they chased
in the dark. He told me the hounds had been torn
in two.

                                                  John Green
                                          The Sasquatch File

March 1973:

HUGE CREATURE RISES OUT OF
GRASSY FIELD

That big, hairy thing has been seen again east of
Lancaster . . . the giant monster that appears only
at night. This time it possibly is responsible for
wounding two dogs and scaring a 19-year-old girl
into hysterics.

                                                Chuck Wheeler
                  Lancaster, Calif., *Daily Ledger Gazette*

May 1975:

Hoopa Indian Reservation, Hoopa Valley,
California, location of numerous Bigfoot
sightings.
During the night, the family dog started raising
an awful ruckus. Suddenly there was a loud thud
on the side of the house and the dog quit barking.
Thinking it might have been the house contracting
after the heat of the day, they didn't go out and
check. However, the next morning when they went

out, there lay the dog beside the house, dead. Something had thrown him against the house with such force that it caved part of the siding in. His head was split open from the impact.

Personal Correspondence from:
W. J. Vogel
Staff Fire Control Officer
Yakima Indian Reservation
Yakima, Washington

It was in this rather gruesome manner that the creatures introduced themselves to the Stone family early in 1974. It was to become a terrifying acquaintanceship. Both in their late twenties, Andrew Stone, an Apache-Comanche Indian, his wife, Hilda, a full-blooded Sioux, and their infant son, Michael, were just getting settled in their new home in Littlerock, California. Many of the cabins in that resort area directly across from the dam were not rented at that time of the year. The fishing boats had been pulled out of the water, turned over, and stacked for the winter. Few people stopped to eat at the small coffee shop-general store. Farther up the canyon, the narrow road was closed because of snow. But because of the excellent fishing, boating, and campground facilities there in the foothills of the San Gabriel Mountains, latecomers would find few vacant campsites during summer months.

Both raised on a reservation in Arizona, the Stones were no strangers to the creature called Bigfoot. The old Indians told tales about him kidnapping Indian women and children. Andrew and Hilda Stone did not ridicule the legends of the old ones. They were a proud family, proud of their heritage. They just didn't anticipate the creature would be existing in the mountains behind their new residence.

Their initial warning that all was not well was in twenty-month-old Michael's reaction to his crib being placed under the bedroom window. "He went into hysterics, screaming and crying, and Andy and I would rock him and he'd quiet down until we tried to put him back under that window," Hilda Stone said. "He had never acted this way at bedtime before. It was like he sensed something outside that window and we finally had to put his crib in another part of the room."

The second evening, the family dog, a tiny Puli, went wild, scratching frantically at the door to be let out. The Stones had wanted to keep the dog fairly confined until he was more familiar with his new surroundings, but eventually they had to succumb to the dog's insistent clamor. He raced quickly around the side of the cabin toward the mountains and was out of sight.

The Puli never returned. They found his dismembered body on the side of the water tank to the rear of the cabin. "He was torn apart, torn to shreds, his head way over there, his tail yards away. Coyotes don't do that! They eat the remains!" Hilda Stone said, her dark eyes reflecting the horror of the remembered scene.

Andrew Stone wondered if it was his fault, if he had encouraged the creatures to come down from the canyons by using his "wounded rabbit" varmint caller. Stone was confident of his ability to track and hunt, and while he left his shotgun in the cabin, he enjoyed perfecting his talent of luring forest predators in. He was soon to realize the "predators" coming closer and closer to the cabin each night were not normal wildlife.

Events were to happen rapidly. A large catch of fish Stone had tied on a stringer and placed at a twelve-foot-high level on a nearby telephone pole disappeared. The stringer was found at the base of the pole, the knots untied. The ladder he had used remained chained at the side of the cabin. The "thief" had left his calling card —immense three-toed footprints led from the pole into the thicket of the mountains.

There would be those strange, still evenings when the crickets would not chirp and the frogs at the lake would stop their croaking. The Stones, sitting on the front porch, would have the overpowering sensation that they were being watched. And then the screams would start echoing through the canyons.

Hilda Stone described them as "A crying, a horrible noise like a woman screaming."

"Bigfoot make different sounds. Sometimes they whistle like an owl—a high-pitched whistle. Maybe they're calling one another," Andrew Stone said. "And sometimes they snort. Another cry we hear sounds like *Mama* but not the way a human would say it. One night the cry kept getting louder and louder. The neighborhood dogs were going frantic, trying to break their leashes. Then *something* slammed the house so hard, it knocked all the knickknacks off the wall. I told Hilda it was a jet because I didn't want to scare her."

It was now March, and returning from some marketing in town, the Stones were driving up the winding canyon road toward the cabin. It was late afternoon, and as the car rounded a curve, they saw a black, hairy form standing in the shallow stream on their left.

"He looked like he was scooping something out of the water, maybe fishing," Hilda recalled.

"Hilda saw it first, but we didn't want to say anything to each other because the other would think we were crazy. It looked about twelve feet tall," Andrew Stone recalled.

Still the creatures came closer to the Stones' cabin. The Stones had gotten another dog, which they named Sunday, an alert mixed terrier that they kept in the house at night to afford Hilda Stone some illusion of protection. In frail health, her doctor had ordered tranquilizers for her increased nervousness. She knew she couldn't confide the reasons for her anxieties. The Stones had once attempted to relate what was happening to some of the locals, but they were laughed at. They didn't know if they were ridiculed because they talked about a creature no one believed in or because they were Indians. They decided it was better not to talk about it.

As the weather grew warmer, tourists began frequenting the area's campgrounds along the stream. In an effort to avoid being seen, the creatures would, under cover of darkness, come down out of the mountains to the water tank at the rear of the Stones' cabin. The tank had a long connecting pipe that, when lowered, would produce a trickle of water sufficient to drink. Yet if the pipe was not turned to its upright position, the water supplying the resort would eventually run out.

Many times, in the predawn hours, the Stones would hear the harsh, metallic clanging of the pipe being slammed back up against the water tank. Andrew Stone would grab a flashlight and run out, to catch a glimpse of eyes glowing red in the reflected light. In the morning, three-toed tracks measuring up to nineteen inches long would be discovered. "His foot is real wide in front and the toes are very large," Andrew Stone said. "The prints are flat, like he doesn't have an arch, and I think he's smart, a lot more intelligent than we think he is, and sometimes tries to cover up his tracks."

On a twilight evening in the spring, as Hilda Stone went to the rear of the cabin to dump the trash, she came face to face with the white one, stooped over drinking from the hose.

"It had hair like an old lady, long and stringy and sort of a dirty white. Its eyes were deep set, and in the few seconds that we stared at each other I could see it had fangs, two coming down from the top jaw and two coming up from the bottom. Its nose was flat like Negroid, and it was definitely a female because she had breasts. Then it ran up the hill on two legs and the odor about it was strong and smelly, a wild odor like a goat or something."

Andrew Stone would describe the odor as something like possum urine, a stench that would linger in the air or on any object the creatures touched for several hours.

Thus far, the creatures hadn't attempted to molest them in any way, but the Stones discussed the old legends—the tales about Bigfoot kidnapping Indian women and children. Were they only stories? Their funds were very limited, based on a small disability pension Andrew Stone received from bullet wounds suffered while on duty as a law-enforcement officer. The cabin rent was nominal and the climate ideal for Hilda Stone's health.

Had the family known about ex-logger, Sasquatch-hunter Rod Puller's opinion, they might have left the area sooner. Puller, a Bellingham, Washington, researcher was, at this same time, teaching a course on Sasquatch at Fairhaven, a division of Western Washington State College. He questioned whether the Sasquatch or Bigfoot was as harmless as some people asserted—like a big, friendly teddy bear. He believed that unexplained disappearances of people in the forests of various parts of the country might have involved the creature. Having sighted several of the giant humanoids himself, Puller was to confirm the various vocalizations heard in other states in an interview with Ted Van Arsdol, staff writer for the *Columbian,* Vancouver, Washington, on March 20, 1974.

The Sasquatch makes a wide variety of noises, according to Puller. Some are imitations of other noises, such as coyote howls or cougar screams, he declared.

One of the noises which Puller contends are made by the Sasquatch are like "yelling or cussing in Oriental language, really weird, a singsong." The Bellingham man also states that he has heard noises like chimpanzees, and growling, which he attributes to the Bigfoot.

For the Stones, it became a war of nerves, waiting for the almost nightly ritual of rocks to be thrown at their cabin roof from some place, anticipating the dogs to start their howling as the creature moved through the canyons, and always the dread of that inhuman wail, a sound that would awaken little Michael and start his frenzied, fearful crying.

Andrew Stone would question the only other family renting a cabin in the resort. "Didn't you hear that scream last night?" Yes, they had. Probably hippies on dope, camping in the hills. Maybe a coyote or something. They didn't know. They didn't *want* to know.

And Bigfoot moved in closer. Andrew Stone sat watching television. It was a warm night and the windows had been opened. It wasn't something he heard but rather a feeling, like being watched. As he turned toward the window to look outside, an oversized form was silhouetted in the screen.

"I could see the color of his face. His skin was a sandy brown," Stone said. "Now, I'm six feet tall and my window stands higher than me. He was bending over to peek in, so I estimate he was about nine feet tall, built like a barn. There was a little hair on the cheekbones and the hairline was low, almost to his eyes."

The creature's immense hand, placed on the screen, revealed only four fingers with black claws. Andrew Stone could not recall seeing a thumb. It was a brief encounter, lasting only a moment but enough to warn Andrew that maybe next time, Bigfoot might decide to walk in through the front door. The dog, Sunday, had not barked but shivered violently under a chair. Stone woke his sleeping wife and son and drove to a motel for the night.

In some manner, this sandy-colored creature had not really frightened Stone. There had been no feeling of hostility, merely curiosity. Not so with the huge black hair-covered one they had seen standing in the stream. The feeling from him was one of malevolence.

"I get really nervous, superspooked, when the black one is around. I was out looking at the ridge the other night and my stomach started feeling like there were butterflies in it. I looked across at the other ridge and the black one was standing there and I knew he was looking at me!"

Fear and nervousness only about the gigantic black creature. Was this really a power play that Andrew Stone could sense, a mute challenge of two males vying for who would be the mate of the Indian woman or who would raise the Indian child?

Andrew Stone did not believe the Bigfoot creature to be an animal, but, rather, that once, long ago, an Indian band, large in stature, had chosen to live in the wilds or perhaps underground in abandoned mines, slowly evolving strength, speed, and hair as their new environment dictated. Thus, in his attitude, there was a live-and-let-live type of policy toward the Bigfoot, perhaps even an instinctive kinship toward what he believed was once an ancient Indian tribe.

But the strain on Hilda Stone, fearing for the safety of their child, began to take its toll. They made plans to relocate. It was then that the most extraordinary of all the already alarming incidents occurred.

It was now late June. Andrew Stone had fallen asleep watching television on the couch in the front room when Hilda shook him awake with a finger at her lips warning him to be silent. The front door knob was jiggling. It was 3:30 A.M. Stone sprang to his feet rapidly, grabbing for his shotgun while his wife unlatched the locked bolt. With his gun concealed behind the door, Stone slowly opened the door halfway.

Standing not on the porch but in the dirt beyond it were two clean-cut young men, estimated in their late teens. They said simultaneously, "We don't want to be hurt!"

That struck the Indian as a rather odd thing to say, especially when the boys could not possibly see his shotgun. "Most people, when they walk up to your house at night, would say something like 'Gee, I hate to bother you,' or something like that. And you'd think they would knock instead of jiggling the door."

Hilda Stone held the trembling Sunday, who usually would be barking loudly at someone's approach. The dog was behaving abnormally, almost with the same mute terror as when the sandy-colored Bigfoot peered through the window.

The visitors announced that they had run out of gas some seven miles down the road, had seen the phone booth outside the resort store, and as the Stones' porchlight was on, wanted to borrow a dime to call someone to bring them some gas. They said they would return the dime promptly after aid came.

Something wasn't registering as true, as the former law-enforcement man observed the boys clearly in the seventy-five-watt porch light. Their clothes were spotless. "Have you ever seen spanking new clothes out of a store? Like that!" Stone would later relate. "And their shoes were a shiny black patent leather with round toes but without a speck of dust on them! And I'm wondering how they could have walked seven miles down a filthy, dusty road without getting their shoes dirty?"

Andrew Stone told them to wait a moment, closed the door, and went to get a dime. His wife continued to hold the shivering dog. Stepping out onto the porch, Stone carefully placed the dime into the outstretched palm of one of the boys. . . .

"And I didn't feel his hand! I was very deliberate to get it right into his hand as I didn't want it to drop in the dirt and get lost because it was the only dime I had. There was nothing there! Like I hadn't even done it!" the puzzled man stated.

Closing the door, he sat down on the couch for only a few seconds, then jumped to his feet. "I realized there was no light in the phone booth and thought I'd better give the guys a flashlight so they could see where they were going. I went out the door with the flashlight in my hand—and they were gone!

"That walk down the hill to the phone booth is a good two hundred yards and I should have been able to see them, whichever direction they went. They had just disappeared!"

Stone walked down to the road, looking all around, but the boys had vanished. "They were nowhere around. *Nowhere.* There were no cars, no noise, the crickets weren't going, the frogs weren't croaking, and I got the eeriest feeling I ever felt!"

In relating this story, Hilda Stone interjected, "It sounds like we were dreaming, but we were wide awake! And Andy doesn't drink! And they never brought back our dime!"

Although Andrew Stone has gone over and over the incident in his mind and remembers what the boys were wearing in detail—the color of their hair and so on—one additional fact haunts him. He cannot recall seeing the eyes of the visitors. And the face of the dark-haired boy remains a blur in his memory.

"Spanking new clothes" and shiny black shoes that should have been dust-covered after a seven-mile walk along the canyon road and up to the Indian's cabin which is unpaved. The dog's reaction of abject fear. A hand without solid, physical properties. And their instant disappearance.

The question must be raised. Were they "men" at all? Had Hilda and Andrew Stone seen a projected thought form, hypnotically induced by the creatures? Had the black-haired "boy" been, in reality, the immense black creature, coming in for a closer, final look as he knew the Indian family would be moving shortly?

A far-out theory perhaps, but ancient Indian legends and other unorthodox events occurring throughout the Antelope Valley during this time led researchers to suspect that the mind of the Bigfoot might indeed possess this telepathic-hypnotic capability. That and something more—the creature was trying to communicate. Was the message, "We don't want to be hurt"?

5

The Psychic Elements

While Captain Ken Coon of the Lancaster Sheriff's Office in southern California, himself a veteran Bigfoot tracker, took the majority of sighting reports flooding into his office that spring of 1973 seriously, many of his men did not. They didn't believe in such a creature in the first place, and in the second place, what was "it" doing in the desert, crossing the street in front of cars—and in the daytime to boot!

"Boy, did I get a razzing from the cops," says John Parkhurst, a high-school student at the time. "I still don't like to talk about it because people laugh at you. The one thing I can say is *I know* what I saw that day. It's never going to get out of my mind!"

Driving east down Avenue J toward his family's ranch on that crisp, slightly overcast April morning, John Parkhurst initially thought what he was seeing was one of the burned, black trees that lined the road on his right.

Until one large "tree" took a step and stood in the middle of the road.

The giant's head was described as peaked, like a "bullet" at the top, sloping down into massive shoulders. It had a small head in proportion to its bulky body, which was covered with black hair. Rather than turning its head to look at the car approaching it at 55 mph, it turned its full upper torso.

"I was like a football field away when I first saw it," the student recalls. "I couldn't believe it! I was like . . . paralyzed! I didn't hit the brakes. I kept going!"

Then, with the speeding car less than 100 yards from it, the black, eight-foot-tall behemoth took one more step, was across the road and out of sight in the desert. A shaky John Parkhurst stepped on the gas and tore out of there.

There had been earlier sightings in this region of the Antelope Valley, such as the mysterious Ragman of Palmdale. "Like a dummy, I ignored that while it was going on, as I thought from the name it was some poor bum the teenagers were bothering," the now-retired Ken Coon writes from Colville, Washington. "Apparently it was a big, hairy, ragged-looking, man-thing seen in the foothills above Palmdale. I should have realized the Antelope Valley was as good a place as any for Bigfooting, but you must realize that during most of the years that I was involved, I thought Bigfoot was strictly an inhabitant of the Northwest woods."

But now, in view of the many creature reports crossing his desk, the captain soon began to surmise that southern California had its share of Bigfoot—and more than one. He investigated the John Parkhurst incident. Footprints were found, one well-defined eighteen-inch-long one with five toes, measuring eight inches across the top and six inches across the heel. A small brush of sage was mashed down as the creature stepped on it.

Yet Captain Coon was puzzled about one factor in the report: "I went to the spot, and although I remember a shallow wash, some brush, and a few Joshua trees, there was nothing to hide an eight-foot-tall giant in just a few seconds. Could he have just disappeared?"

There was the remains of an old reservoir up a dusty access road in the vicinity, however. "Just a big hole in the ground," John Parkhurst said. "I went up that road that night and looked in. It might have once been an old coyote den, but now there were a lot of cobwebs and spiders so nothing large had been sleeping there. Even though I was still scared, *it was like something was making me do it!"*

Was this the same creature that the three Marines reported seeing run across Avenue J that March night, a "big, dark creature about eight feet tall" causing them to halt their vehicle with a screech of the brakes and tires skidding? The Marines were even more upset when the Sheriff's Office didn't get excited about the incident.[1]

About a week later, the officer on duty would tell Bill Hawkins of Hawkins Flying Service, just off Avenue J, that what his daughter had seen was probably a bear. Hawkins didn't think so.

Kim, age nineteen, was returning to the Hawkins trailer about 2:30 A.M. after baby-sitting in Lancaster. As she got out of her car, she expected her dogs, tails wagging, to greet her as usual. They were always there, never absent from their bed beneath the trailer. From behind the trailer, a whining, plaintive cry or moan was heard and Kim walked in that direction, thinking that perhaps the dogs were hurt or in trouble.

It was full moon, light enough to read a wristwatch by. Then suddenly, from the tall grass, a huge form slowly arose, almost as if awakening from sleep. It stood on two legs, almost eight feet tall and was completely covered with hair except for portions of the face. As the "being" ran away on two legs, Kim ran in the other direction, pounding frantically on the trailer door to be let in.

"Kim has no fear of the dark or coming home alone," her father said. "She has lived here all her life and is not afraid of the fields and is not the scary type."

But that night, inside the trailer, his daughter would be hysterical, repeating over and over again in shock, "Big . . . big . . . big."

Still more Bigfoot reports came into the Sheriff's Office, now from campgrounds in the valley's high country, the nearby San Gabriel Mountains. One of these had been made by three students attempting to enjoy their Easter vacation backpacking. It hadn't quite worked out as planned.

Patches of snow lay on the ground at the site known as Big Rock, the last camping facility at the end of the winding canyon. All in their late teens, Richard Engels, Brian Goldojarb, and Willie Roemermann had been there two days—the camp's only residents. It was on the third night that Willie Roemermann began acting strangely, like he wanted to get out of there but wasn't sure why. He was somehow uneasy. Perhaps it was just boredom, but his friends didn't think so, because Willie kept looking nervously toward the dense trees in the mountains surrounding them. His attitude was one of listening. Since they were all experienced outdoorsmen, familiar with the minor discomforts of backpacking and the sometimes foreboding moods of the forest at night, the student's behavior was highly unusual.

"Willie was *really* insistent about leaving, inventing lame excuses about getting a sore throat because his sleeping bag wasn't warm enough," Brian Goldojarb said. "Rich and I said *no way,* we had planned to stay there three days and we were going to stay!"

Roemermann was to win the heated argument, however, as it was his '53 Chevy pickup they had come in. He threatened to leave them there without a ride home, not suspecting that the "something" he sensed, making him edgy, would be waiting just down the canyon road.[2]

Driving slowly past the Sycamore Flats campground at the lower portion of the canyon, Willie Roemermann thought he glimpsed something huge and dark standing near the campground entrance. He quickly dismissed it from his mind as a shadow from a tree, a product of his unwarranted fears about the area. His two companions, riding in the bed with their backs to the cab, thought they *had* to be seeing things. From the campground had emerged a tremendous figure that loped with ease down the center of the road behind them, matching the 20-mph speed of the pickup. The figure was clearly silhouetted in the light from the full moon behind it. One arm swung loosely while the other was held up against the body as if carrying something.

The head was a very pronounced conical shape. There was no evidence of a neck. "The impression we had was that it was thin but not frail," Brian Goldojarb said. "The head of this thing wasn't missing the overhanging sycamore branches by more than four or five feet, so it was tall!"

The driver of the truck, not looking in his rearview mirror, saw nothing, so he continued down the canyon road. His two friends in the back had, by this time, reached for their flashlights just as the truck rounded a curve. They waited . . . but the immense apparition did not reappear.

They stopped to eat at a small café in the nearby town of Pearblossom, and Engels and Goldojarb excitedly related to Roemermann the fantastic thing they had observed. They decided to report this to the Sheriff's Office. They didn't drink; they hated dopers; and they *knew* they had to make someone believe them. It was with some astonishment when filing their report that the officer advised the boys there had already been five "monster" or Bigfoot reports coming out of that area in the past week.

While too frightened to return to the canyon that evening, the three went back to Sycamore Flats in the morning, to search for possible tracks left by the creature. "The dirt was pretty hard around the campground," they said. "We found some strange prints but not like complete tracks, so we followed these down past the campground where there was a drainage ditch. And this is where we found his footprints and where he had apparently been crouched down."

It wasn't the fact that the lean prints measured almost nineteen inches long that held the boys spellbound as they looked at them. It was the fact that the creature apparently had only three toes!

Their lives would change. The Bigfoot hunt was on. The research had top priority. Weekends, every school holiday, and the majority of the summer was spent around the area, searching for additional footprints, making plaster casts of fresh, three-toed "finds," talking to the townspeople (the majority of whom were most reticent to discuss the subject), questioning tourists in the campgrounds to inquire if they had heard or seen anything strange (until the ranger advised them that they were making nuisances of themselves and had to stop walking through the hills with flashlights at all hours of the night).

The students had cut out a cardboard figure simulating the thing following the truck that March evening, sprayed it black, and stood it under the overhanging sycamore branches to estimate its height. From the road to the lowest branch measured a little better than sixteen feet. Brian Goldojarb stood behind the cardboard figure to brace it as Richard Engels walked down the road to the place the truck had been when the creature was sighted.

"Man, that's it! that's *it!*" he yelled, jumping up and down with excitement. The boys exchanged positions for a comparative opinion and Goldojarb would concur with his friend. *The cardboard form stood an incredible eleven feet in height!*

Thus the Angeles Sasquatch Association was born. There were no dues, no membership, no meetings, and no president. The informal, unstructured group would mail postcards throughout the Antelope Valley which read, "To report a Bigfoot sighting, call this number." The persons who would be welcome in the ASA had to have a sincere desire for the research, which included the ability to stay up most of the night listening for sounds, overcoming their fears about hiking the canyons in the dark to search for fresh tracks, and being able to chip in on the gas to get the seventy miles out there.

It was a working field group that would learn as they went along, lacking any Bigfoot tracker's manual to be guided by. They dismissed any ideas of trying to interest men of science after being advised over the telephone to get a field guide book on animal tracks (Curator's Office, Los Angeles Zoo) and "maybe they are giant three-toed sloth tracks" (County Museum of Natural History). No one offered to look at the plaster casts.

They discovered it was far better to use hair spray rather than talcum powder to photograph the footprints. This would set the soil in preparation for making a cast, which, ground permitting, took about ten pounds of plaster. Standard equipment became a snake-bite kit, tape recorders, walkie-talkies, yardsticks, cameras, spotlights, a Citizens Band radio, plaster, water jugs, a bucket, as well as a cheerful optimism when countless night-long vigils produced nothing.

A "baby" three-toed print had been found, lacking in arch span between toes and heel. And then there was Clubfoot, so named because of the bone distortion of one of his nineteen-inch-long feet. Because of this distinguishing feature, Clubfoot was easy to identify and track as he made his way down the canyon to the ripe pears in the orchards below.

Often, the group had heard the creatures call to one another; a measured whistle of three notes, rising in pitch with the last note sustained. The ASA perfected the call. Had they been less familiar with forest wildlife, they might have assumed it to be a birdcall. But now they were to discover something seemingly impossible about the Bigfoot creature. While they could hear his footfalls and his heavy breathing nearby, sometimes they couldn't *see* him!

It was early 1974. Four of the ASA stood at the edge of the Big Rock Campground. It was a moonless night. From a ridge in the distance to their left came the first whistle. They heard a responding whistle up the inky canyon road. Richard Engels answered with his best imitation. And within sixty seconds the group was to sense they were surrounded. For with Bigfoot comes a special kind of "feeling," the kind that makes the hair on your arms stand up and the back of your neck prickle.

Now close in, from behind a tree some fifty yards away and in the direction of the ridge came another eerie whistle, to be immediately answered in kind by something on the road directly across the campground from where they stood. And, scant yards behind the tense but alert trackers, from the dense trees on the hillside came the third quick high-pitched whistle. The group froze . . . and waited. Suddenly they saw glowing red eyes, about ten feet from the ground, peering at them through a large, thick bush at the edge of the dry creekbed.

A girl screamed, unable to contain her fear. Engels, flashlight and camera in hand, ran quickly around the bush to see . . . *nothing*. He searched the ground for tracks, but the rocky creekbed permitted no such confirmation.

The ASA researched the region's history. It was said the Mojave Desert Indians had legends about the "old people" who were there before them, having secret places where magic was performed—an aboriginal people of which little was known.[3] The group wondered: was some of this "magic" created by hypnotism? After the initial sighting by Engels and Goldojarb, strange, dancing lights would be spotted driving up the canyon. When they were in the Big Rock area, pinpoint lights would circle their cars. Was this "flicker hypnosis," used in experiments by the military, suggesting that their minds were already under control, their visual senses blocked by "something" even before they arrived at the site of the evening's proposed stakeout? What caused those lights? UFOs? The ASA formed no theories but continued to investigate.

Bruce Morgan and Willie Roemermann attempted an experiment outside Sycamore Flats. Although there had been no recent reported sightings, the group's efforts continued to locate freshly made tracks, indicating the creatures were returning to specific spots, like around the water tank just over the ridge from the campground. It seemed a likely spot to attempt a highly unlikely test.

Morgan, a college science major, kept a healthy, skeptical attitude about the paranormal aspect he'd heard about the Bigfoot creature. As they sat in the darkened car on a small access road, Morgan held a tape recorder in his lap, the exterior mike extended

Bigfoot

outside the window. They saw pinpoints of lights zipping about the canyon on the way to their destination, but Morgan kept an open mind about the ability of these to produce auditory or visual sensory blocks that would enable the creature to seem invisible. The boys saw and heard nothing that warm evening, but at one point, Morgan exclaimed, "Willie, there's something cold around my hand. It's freezing!"

When the tape was replayed later, definite footfalls could be heard approaching the car. There were sounds of heavy, deep breathing and then a clicking noise that could be produced only by "something" deliberately touching the microphone.

Then, in the mountains at Big Rock, late August, the science student experienced a phenomenon that none of his objectivity could explain. It was midnight. Another experiment was being attempted, using psychic Cinthia McQuillan in the hopes that, through her powers of extrasensory preception, some telepathic rapport might be established with the creatures. Those same flashing lights had been seen emanating from a circular source above the tops of the skyline.

A small group composed of three people stood talking quietly as the psychic, sitting on a tree stump, meditated several yards away. Bruce Morgan headed over to the campground's outhouse and stopped, staring in disbelief. For there, behind the weathered, wooden structure crouched a light-colored figure.

"It was on its hands and knees, weaving back and forth!" Morgan said. "The hair was shaggy and white. Even in that position, it was six feet tall! It seemed to be looking straight at me. I didn't see the eyes reflecting, which has been reported before, although we had observed two glowing luminescent disks in the dark earlier that night which could be described as eyes.

"This thing had long slender arms and a slender torso, which didn't qualify it as any kind of bear I knew about. I should have taken a picture, but I estimated I didn't have enough light."

Then something even more bizarre occurred. Morgan had observed the white, hairy form for about eight seconds before walking rapidly over to the nearby group engaged in quiet conversation.

"Willie! Come here! I see something!" he whispered loudly, urgently.

Willie turned to look briefly at Morgan and then turned back, his attention focused on the group. Morgan couldn't believe his friend's reaction—his blank stare as if he didn't see him. They had often hunted together and each would immediately respond to the other's call. No one in the group had reacted. It was as if he, Morgan, wasn't even there! He returned to look again behind the outhouse, but the creature had disappeared.

And Willie Roemermann, although he had briefly turned to look at his friend when he was calling to him, *does not remember seeing him!*

Had the psychic's trancelike state temporarily nullified the visual screen the creatures appear to be able to place around themselves? Had Bruce Morgan been in close enough proximity to the psychic to see through this veil and glimpse the white creature? Had this, in turn, placed *him* within this mysterious "zone of invisibility" so that the group, standing a mere nine feet away, did not see him or hear his urgent call? Or perhaps it had merely been an apparition?

"What I saw was three-dimensional!" Morgan insists.

And what singer-composer Terry Albright almost ran over on that same canyon road was definitely physical and three-dimensional. The twenty-eight-year-old musician had recently joined the ASA on another of their routine stakeouts in the mountains. That evening, there had been no indication—no cries, whistles, fresh prints, or "feelings"—that Bigfoot was around. Two of the group's cars had already made the boulevard stop halfway down the canyon as they headed for home, their taillights receding in the distance.

Albright waited and then revved up his motor, wanting to see how fast his new car would corner down the winding road. Willie Roemermann and Rich Engels followed him but slowly, as their vehicle was considerably older. They heard the harsh squeal of Albright's tires against the blacktop and then . . . an

ominous silence. The musician's joy of "cornering" was
known to the group.

"He's gone and done it this time, Willie!" Engels said
with some concern. "Gone right over the damn cliff!
Let's hurry!"

As they rounded the curve, Albright's car stood
broadside across the narrow road. The driver, with
ashen face and in a state of shock, related the following.
As he sped around the turn, a seven-foot-tall, black,
hair-covered form was just stepping down off the shoulder at his right.

"The hair wasn't thick but scraggly, like moth-eaten,"
the trembling man related. "God, I almost hit him! I
could see him plainly in the headlights. His face was
dark and leathery and so was the skin showing through
in spots where there wasn't any body hair. He might
have been a tall, lean Negro basketball player except
that, in just *one* step, he cleared the road and was down
the ridge. That's got to be a stride of thirteen feet!"

A search of the incline at the left indicated fresh
scuffle marks from the creature's descent. They played
their flashlights across the creekbed and mountains but
saw no movement. It was surmised that the creature had
waited until the first two cars were out of sight, standing silently in the brush on the side of the hill. Because
of the curve in the road, it could not have seen Albright's lights approaching or anticipated the speed
at which the vehicle was moving.

A Bigfoot of the same description was encountered by
Neil Forn and Rich Engels in another portion of the
Antelope Valley in September—an incident with more
menacing overtones. Having learned of the earlier sightings along Avenue J, the youths drove to the extreme
eastern end of the street, which ends in harsh, almost
moonlike terrain. Craggy stone buttes dot the landscape.
It was a moonless night, and the stars were brilliant
against the dark, desert sky. Flashlights in hand, they
searched for tracks.

They walked about a quarter of a mile from the
road, and climbing a ridge, Forn noticed a small pile
of rocks stacked in a neat pyramid fashion, centered on

a large flat rock. The blond student did not know of Sasquatch researcher-writer John Green's documentation of this curious trait of rock stacking.[4] As Forn approached the mound of rocks, an eerie feeling came over him.

"I could sense a hostility, like *something* didn't want us there!" he said. "It was like we were just barely being tolerated. And I had this feeling that if I touched those rocks, it was going to kill me!"

Engels had already experienced the overpowering sensation that they were being watched. He caught up to Forn, now making his way back down the ridge.

"Where are you going, Neil?"

"I'm getting a *bad* feeling," Forn replied. "Let's get away from these rocks!"

As Engels asked him exactly which rocks he was referring to, he simultaneously turned around, the beam from his flashlight framing a dark form standing on the rocky crag above them. The figure was described as about seven feet in height, lean, with shaggy black hair covering the body. The head was conical-shaped. It ducked quickly behind some boulders, too rapidly for cameras to be reached. Due to the bad "vibes" emanating from this creature—the unmistakable cold hatred it projected—the trackers decided it would be more prudent to wait for daylight to investigate.

Later, in the vicinity of the encounter, three-toed, narrow, fifteen-inch footprints were found, in keeping with the described height and weight of this particular Bigfoot.

If, as John Green claims, the Sasquatch will eat rodents, picking up rocks to smell them for scent and then neatly stacking them in piles, it is probable that the ASA searchers had inadvertently infringed on this particular creature's hunting grounds, and it wasn't happy about it. Or perhaps these reported stone pyramids represented "posted" territorial boundaries advising others of the species that this terrain was already "taken."

It has been questioned how a being of such huge proportions can feed in what appears to be barren desert, but the Mojave abounds with ground squirrels, kangaroo rats, jackrabbits, and coyotes. The shell remains of two small desert tortoises were discovered near the stacked-rock pyramid, the fleshy parts eaten away. A man can stand on the tough shell of a live tortoise with no injury to it. The two specimens found had had their protective covering broken by some tremendous force that split the shell into deep fractures radiating from the center.

Newcomers to the Angeles Sasquatch Association team, sometimes overzealous in their attempts to contribute by pointing out vague scuffle marks in the dirt, were quickly advised that anything less than a distinct five- or three-toed footprint with a stride that could be measured was unacceptable. They learned not to jump to conclusions about sounds in the desert night, assuming every noise to be that of the Bigfoot. They learned to distinguish between the vocalizations of coyotes and cougars. They had to learn to instantly obey a whispered "Be quiet!" They learned the disappointments of all-night vigils without anything occurring. And they had to learn to keep an open mind about the ambiguities of what seemed to be paranormal.

"It was like he would know we were coming before we got there!" Rich Engels said, referring to several attempts with professional, scientific persons with specialized night-vision equipment who had offered their services.

Physicist Neil Davis and Jack Carroll, photographer, came from San Diego to join the ASA in a stakeout in a promising area—near Avenue J, where several sets of three-toed prints indicating a routine path had been located. Seven people took their positions on top of ridges, behind bushes, in gullies—various vantage points of observation. They waited. Nothing happened. Even more peculiar in this coyote-infested region, not one bayed all night. The ground squirrels, always seen scurrying throughout the sagebrush, seemed to have vanished. The desert was silent . . . too silent.

There would be another occasion with animal-tele-path Fred Kimball and psychiatrist Dr. Robert Jordan, this time for a stakeout at Big Rock, an area always

THE BIGFOOT MYSTERY

UNEXPLAINED PHENOMENA OF OUR TIME . . .

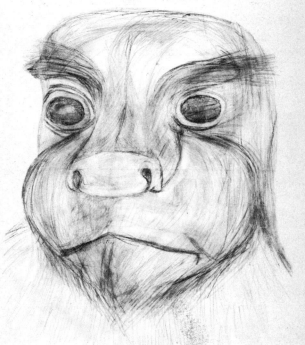

Eyewitness drawing of Bigfoot
roaming the Cascade Mountains, Oregon.
By Thomas E. Smith, June 1972.

Voiceprint: an electronically produced graphic presentation of spoken words or parts of a spoken word which shows the frequency, amplitude, and rate of speaking of a voice, and which can be used for purposes of identification.

(Upper) Actual voiceprint of Bigfoot resembling the vocalization "Gob-a-gob-a-gob, ugh, muy-tail."

(Lower) A human voice attempts to imitate the same Bigfoot utterance, but fails conspicuously. The voiceprints show that the Bigfoot voice is not human, nor is it the articulation of any known animal as indicated by the glottal break in "muy-tail." (Prepared at experimental sound laboratories, the University of California at Davis. Bigfoot voiceprints are available to scientists and accredited institutions, applying to Bantam Books, Inc.)

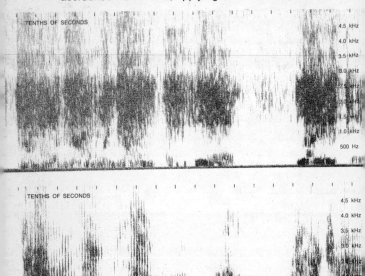

Bigfoot trackers Warren Johnson (left) and Ron McDowell pour plaster for a cast of 18-inch five-toed footprint. The track was discovered in northern California in 1974.

—The Authors

—The Authors

Author Alan Berry's own foot-long boot alongside the cast of one of many footprints he found in the snow in 1974 and 1975.

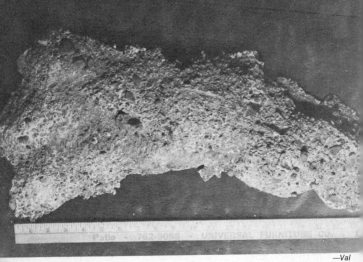

Cast of "Clubfoot," the Bigfoot nicknamed by the Angeles
Sasquatch Association of Southern California.

19-inch three-toed footprints located in the San Gabriel
Mountains at the border of the Mojave Desert in 1974.

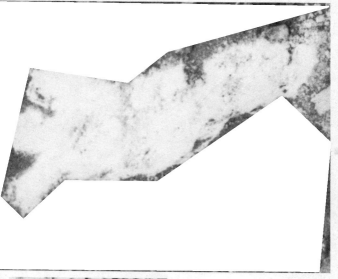

Author Ann Slate with friend.
A man in a gorilla suit
demonstrates the unlikelihood
of a Bigfoot hoax using
theatrical costumes.

Author Alan Berry (left) and fellow Bigfoot-tracker
Warren Johnson seal their Sierra shelter entrance with logs
—a precaution used when the creatures began to stalk them.

—The Authors

Three students—Brian Goldojarb, Richard Engels and
Willie Roemerman (left to right)—and a cardboard
reconstruction of the huge figure that pursued them from
their campsite, loping along after their pickup truck in
Angeles National Forest, southern California, March 1973.

Timbered area on the Yakima Indian Reservation in Washington where mysterious lights have been seen and frightening Bigfoot encounters have occurred.

—Bill Vogel

producing eerie feelings and unwarranted anxieties. That evening, Big Rock Campground would feel as comfortable as a Sunday picnic in the park.

And the middle-aged employee of the Forestry Service nicknamed Doc would have the final laugh. He had often teased Engels and Roemermann for pursuing a mirage. Bigfoot didn't exist, certainly not in his territory, and one of these days, Doc warned, the two boys were going to get in serious trouble with the rangers because of their frequent nighttime explorations.

The ASA founders bided their time, waiting for some unmistakable prints that even old Doc would have to accept. In the fall of 1974 they found them, perfect, recently made three-toed tracks by the water tower over the hill from the Sycamore Flats Campground. Six of the most clearly defined footprints ever located showed the creature's immense stride from the tower down into the gully that led into the mountains. On the canyon road below, Doc's familiar green Forestry truck went by. The boys jumped into their truck and raced to intercept him.

Roemermann later stated, shaking his head in frustration, "We wanted to be doubly sure about showing Doc something he *had* to believe—*good* prints—so we wouldn't make jackasses out of ourselves. We ended up doing just that! We got Doc to come up to the water tower and the tracks were *gone,* like Bigfoot came back and picked them up. Rich and I stared at the ground where they had been, feeling like a couple of jerks."

Had this been an error in observation or judgment? One of the authors, B. Ann Slate, having tracked with the Angeles Sasquatch Association for over twenty months, seriously doubts that Engels and Roemermann had misinterpreted ordinary footprints or tried to build a case on vague markings in the dirt. But what kind of realistic alternatives did this leave? To assume Bigfoot had lurked behind some bush that day, rapidly sweeping away his tracks as the boys drove off to intercept Doc?

There was one other possibility for which the evidence continued to mount, indicating that the creature's telepathic faculties were again at play, exerting some kind of hypnotic influence over the human mind so that they could not "see" the path he had taken up the gully and thus escaping detection.

What was Bigfoot's ultimate destination? Did he dwell in the many natural caves or abandoned mines in the region? Did he hide in undetected and unexplored shelters in the dense pines of the high country? Or, because this area was directly over the vast San Andreas Rift, was he secreted underground, in natural tunnel formations created by the earth's upheavals in the long and distant past?

Because of a unique incident occurring at Big Rock, the ASA had begun to suspect that perhaps their particular three-toed "friends" were subterranean, and perhaps aided by "someone" with some sophisticated technology.

A tape recorder with built-in microphone had been placed on the ground. Nothing could be heard but the sound of the crickets chirping. Yet when the tape was replayed, sounds of machinery were distinctly heard —those resembling a generator or hydroelectric plant in operation but coming from *beneath* their feet. The sounds do not remain consistent but subtly change, as if new "gears" are set in motion. Suddenly the sounds stop. From the tape comes a harsh, almost computer-type voice that whispers something sounding very much like "Keep out! We don't want . . ." And with that, the voice fades.

It was questioned whether the Big Rock area might be an acoustical zone, picking up sounds from elsewhere. But checks with the only installation nearby, a probation camp, indicated that all equipment was shut down nightly at 11:00 P.M. The tape recorder had not been placed on the ground until well after midnight.

Were they standing over "someone's" underground facility or had this been a freak, isolated malfunction of the tape recorder? All attempts to reproduce the "voice" failed. It was not the recorder's spindles creating the sounds. Nor, the ASA would learn, was this to be an isolated case.

In March 1975, from Cedar City, Utah, Dick Millett would write:

My wife and I moved into a mountain cabin 70 miles from Cedar, high in the mountains. Every night at around 11 o'clock, we hear a motor running, but it sounds far away and runs through the night. There is also a mine tunnel close by that has recently been dug further in.

I entered it with a kerosene lamp, and when I came to the part that was the new diggings, the walls lit up like little diamonds. But the owner of the mine has not dug there for some time. He refuses to stay there alone anymore because of strange happenings. Before, he stayed there for years.

One morning I heard heavy footsteps coming toward our cabin, then saw a huge, dark form [move] across the window. I grabbed my gun and threw a cartridge into the chamber as our doorknob turned. Whatever was out there never entered. I slowly opened the door. There was nothing there and I heard no heavy footsteps leaving. Our two dogs were just outside the door but never barked. What puzzles me is there were no footprints of any kind and we have lots of snow here. My Indian friends tell me it is *Newputz,* meaning ghost in their language, and only a few will dare stay in the area overnight.

The sound of the motor we hear runs on the weekends. If the sound was coming from a mining company, it would be shut down on weekends.

Then from Montreal, Quebec, came the following from a hunter who wishes to remain anonymous:

What I am about to tell you is a true story that actually happened to myself and a fellow hunter. We both are members of a Hunting and Fishing Club, 354 miles north of Montreal. Three years ago [1972], we had organized a moose hunt with other members of our club. The plan was that all seven of us were to meet on Saturday at our club.

From there, the following day, we were to be flown in pairs to lakes further north.

René and myself were chosen for the first flight. Due to our small plane, the trip was to be done in two flights because of weight problems. Each party was to spend nine days at each location and every second day, the plane would return to see if all was well. Well, as you know, all best plans sometimes are not realized.

We were flown to our destination at 1:00 P.M. On the first trip, all that we could carry was the tent, our sleeping bags, rifles, and one small box of food that contained one loaf of bread, one-half pound of butter, and two small cans of meat. We were flown 80 air miles north of our base camp to a beautiful lake which had signs of moose all over the place.

In October, in the northern country, nighttime comes early and at 4:00 P.M. our plane did not return with the rest of our hunting gear and food. We found out five days later that the plane was grounded due to a severe snowstorm at our base camp. We spent five days and four nights with no cigarettes, no liquor, and only one loaf of bread and two cans of meat. What happened on our first night and the others is an experience that we will never forget.

At 5:00 P.M. night was upon us and since we had no light and no heater with us, the only thing to do was to crawl into our sleeping bags. My partner, René, is a heavy sleeper, and as soon as he was in his bag, he was asleep. I always have trouble falling asleep and this is when I first heard the noise.

As I related in the early part of this letter, our base camp is 354 air miles north of Montreal and we were another 80 air miles further north of our camp. You may appreciate that this far north, there are no towns, no sounds of cars or trains, and there are no commercial airlines that fly over this part of Quebec, so at night, it is so quiet and peaceful you can hear the crackling sound of the pine trees in the cold of the northern night.

The sound I heard seemed to come from the bowels of the earth. It sounded like machinery, the same sound you would hear if you were in an engineering plant. I listened to this sound for five minutes before waking up my partner. He too heard it and we stayed up for two hours listening to it and talking about it. There are no waterfalls in this area and the nearest town is La Tuque, which is 234 miles away.

I can still hear this sound in the back of my mind and it has haunted me ever since.

Subterranean machinery sounds where there should be none . . . tracks that disappear . . . flickering, darting lights in the night sky . . . recorded sounds from "something" that remains invisible. For the Angeles Sasquatch Association, it had begun at Big Rock Campground; thus on February 14, 1975, Willie Roemermann, Richard Engels, and Gary Smith, a twenty-five-year-old Civil Service employee, returned to the remote campsite in the hopes of an encounter with the creature.

They sat quietly around the fire, listening for those familiar whistles and branches cracking indicating Bigfoot was nearby. The winter night was hushed. By 1:00 A.M. the three were tired and cold and began tying their hammocks in the trees, which would keep their bedrolls off the snow-covered ground.

"I had just gotten to sleep over the noise of Willie's snoring when something, I don't know what it was, not a noise, pulled me slowly out of my sleep," Engels said. "I was wide awake, listening, trying to sense what was going on. I heard Willie call my name. I answered him, but he called my name again. Before I could respond, he said, 'If you look at the fire, you'll see something you don't want to see.'

"I quietly untied the string of my sleeping bag and turned to look behind me at what had been our fire, which was now just coals, wondering what Willie was talking about. And *everything went black!*"

The embers of the fire, the sky, the stars, and the mountains—all these were blotted out as, for a moment, Engels went blind. When he turned away, his sight was restored. He called to Willie, but there was no response.

"So I tried again, louder than before but still keeping my voice soft enough so Gary wouldn't wake up."

"What the hell do you want?" Roemermann responded sleepily, his head popping out of his bedroll.

"Why did you tell me to look at the fire?"

"I never said nothing about looking at no fire!"

Abruptly, the third man awoke, yelling, "Something's wrong!" Engels asked him what was wrong. The man was shuddering.

"I don't know. I just can't stop shaking, but I'm not cold. I feel like something else is in my body and mind which shouldn't be there!"

Suddenly the fire flared up, burning as if a fresh piece of wood had been added. It continued to burn brightly for several minutes. Rich Engels could not bring himself to turn around and look at it. He focused his attention on his two friends: Smith, who was still trembling uncontrollably, and Willie, who looked as though he had been hypnotized, staring blankly ahead of him, glassy-eyed.

'Look at the fire, Gary," Engels urged, but the shivering man did not respond.

"My heart was pounding real hard. Something was happening, but I didn't know what. I was holding myself back from looking at that fire, but I didn't know why," Smith said. Nor did Engels understand the dread, the threat that prevented him from turning to look again at the fire, which should have been cold now but was blazing anew.

And unknown to them at the time, while this bizarre incident was in progress, Willie Roemermann's German shepherd dog, some seventy miles away, would be acting strangely, barking loudly and scratching at bedroom doors in an effort to wake the family, as if sensing something.

After thirty agonizing minutes, whatever "it" was, left. The three men felt a calmness, a sense of reality returning, but they were weak and drained of energy. Two complained of flulike symptoms and headaches.

"Was this a show of Bigfoot's powers?" Engels later asked. "Was he standing there by the fire and I didn't *want* to see him or was it a case of spooks and possession? It's something we'll always wonder about."

Ghosts? A psychic force? Or something else, perhaps an attempt by the creatures to telepathically reach the human mind? If so, in this instance, they failed. The three in that campground that winter night had become fearful and disoriented, rejecting the alien, exterior thoughts superimposed on their own.

Yet the Bigfoot creatures had made other attempts at mind-to-mind contact with other human beings, telepathic attempts that had succeeded. . . .

NOTES

1. Chuck Wheeler, *Daily Ledger Gazette* (Lancaster, Calif., March 1973).

2. B. Ann Slate, "Gods from Inner Space," *SAGA* (January 1975).

3. Russ Leadabrand, *Exploring California Byways* (Ward Ritchie Press, 1969).

4. John Green, *On the Track of the Sasquatch* (Agassiz, B.C., Cheam Publishing Ltd., 1968).

6

Astounding Incidents

Sasquatch is the popular name for the human-like monster said to inhabit the rugged mountain areas from British Columbia to California. The Skagit River Indian bands called these creatures See-Atco and explain their origin with this story.

Sometime in the dim past, a warring band from the Nookachamis tribe swept down from the hills and attacked the Utsaladdy Indians. The fierce Nookachamis warriors killed many of the Utsaladdy and forced the survivors to abandon their village.

To escape death, the terror-stricken Utsaladdy climbed into their canoes and paddled across Skagit Bay to the safety of Whidbey Island. They settled on the beach between what is now Oak Harbor and Coupeville, Washington.

Joining with a smaller band of Skagits who inhabited that area, the refugees developed a mysterious form of self-hypnotism that gave them the ability to see in the dark. During daylight hours, they learned to cast a spell on themselves so that they became invisible to all who were not members of their band.

By studying and perfecting this secret hypnotic practice, they slowly evolved into a different people. Their appearance became almost apelike and they grew to be the size of giants. . . .

In more recent times, the Indians say the See-Atco have developed even greater size and strength. With each passing decade, their bodies became more animal-like and covered with longer hair. Through their ancient practice of self-hypnosis, they are said to be so powerful that larger See-Atco can easily uproot the tallest of trees. . . .

Emerson N. Matson
"Legends of the Great Chiefs"

Thirty-year-old Ron Bailey resides in Palmdale, California. A lean, hard-muscled man, Bailey is dedicated to his wife Margaret and their infant son Brian; he is active in his church and content with his job at Rockwell International. On the exterior, he lives what might be called "the normal life." Yet on weekends, armed and accompanied by selected individuals, Bailey tracks the mammoth, hair-covered creature known as Bigfoot. The group has taken the name of the High Desert Sasquatch Research Team. They appear to have some advantage over other Bigfoot investigators, for it seems the hairy colossus is also tracking Ron Bailey.

In 1972, the Palmdale man had never heard of the Indian folktales about a manlike being, and had he, he would have given them scant consideration. That was soon to change on a sweltering summer evening as he drove into his carport at the housing tract where they rented a small cottage. Bailey was instantly on the alert. Special jungle tracking experience for the Force Reconnaissance Marines in Vietnam and Cambodia had provided him with an extensive background of the observation of minute details. He sensed something different and wrong about that night, but what was it?

The silence. Neighborhood dogs should have been

barking, alerting their owners to the car's approach. Crickets should have been chirping. Yet everything was hushed and quiet—a strange quiet.

The light from the next duplex shone into the yard, casting shadows on the large bush behind the carport. It appeared to be swaying slightly as if by the wind. But there was no trace of a breeze to cool that hot desert night. A rotten odor that Bailey compares to "sewage or spoiled apples" was emanating from somewhere near the bush.

"I'm not the scary type, but I made a beeline for the house in no uncertain terms!" the veteran said. Now within the safety of the duplex, he put on the kitchen lights, pulled up the blinds, and looked out. He saw nothing except the big bush, which was no longer moving.

"So, I thought to myself, it's as plain as day. I'm losing my marbles!" Bailey said. "I started to let the blinds down when something grabbed me mentally. I don't know what it was—it's beyond description, but it was literally hypnotizing me! I'm not a dramatic person, or an imaginative one. You could say I'm about as down-to-earth as a doorknob, but I felt like something alien and outside myself was trying to control me."

As the Palmdale man stood transfixed at his window, unable to move a muscle and being commanded mentally from somewhere in the courtyard to continue looking, he saw it. There, standing motionless and relaxed next to the telephone pole in the center of the yard some fifty feet away was a nine-foot black, hairy form. While shadows obscured the giant's face, Bailey felt it was looking directly into his eyes, somehow telepathically, hypnotically urging him to come to it.

Bailey broke out in a profuse sweat as he fought the terrible compulsion that was not his own. For long moments suspended in time, the two stared, the gigantic dark form mentally urging and Bailey mentally resisting but weakening with each passing second.

Then abruptly, as if tired of the game, the hairy figure strode away across the courtyard, disappearing into the inky blackness of the desert night. Bailey's head collapsed with fatigue and relief against the kitchen cupboard. The nightmare was over. It was gone, whatever it was, he thought to himself, wiping beads of moisture from his forehead.

The veteran couldn't have known this was just the beginning. He saw this creature, or others like him, again, and although his formerly "normal" life-style remained the same on the outside, Bailey was now possessed with the fires of curiosity. He had to find this manlike thing who tried to mentally control him . . . and who very nearly succeeded.

The city of Palmdale lies on the westernmost edge of the Great Mojave Desert. The area is known as the Antelope Valley. Bordered on the south by the San Gabriels and on the north by the Tehachapi Mountains, what was once barren desert is now becoming a major aircraft manufacturing and testing center. Here Lockheed of California turns out the world's quietest jetliner, the Tri-Star. Rockwell International will soon begin their new contract for the space-shuttle assembly project. It is also the site of a proposed international airport that, when completed, will encompass over seventeen thousand acres of desert land.

Nearby locations are a haven for recreationists from the Greater Los Angeles area. On holidays, motor homes wind their way up canyon roads to quiet campgrounds in the Angeles National Forest. The whine of engines from motorcycles and dune buggies can be heard on the weekends coming from the buttes and dry lake beds of the high desert.

It seems an unlikely choice of habitat for Bigfoot, yet multiple-witness sightings since the early 1970s throughout Antelope Valley have established his existence in the region. Perhaps he is only migrating through that portion of the desert or perhaps he has always lived there, hidden in the many natural caves and abandoned mines. But as civilization moves into formerly remote areas, the creature is seen more frequently and he angrily protests man's trespassing into his domain.

Mike Pense didn't know he was in anyone else's territory that summer in 1973. It was his day off, and Pense, on his 450 Honda, was doing the thing he like best—riding through the deserted sandy buttes of the Mojave. As the soft sand deepened near the top of a ridge, Pense gunned his motor for additional speed. The powerful bike made a deafening roar. At the top, near an old mine, he shut off the motor to relax and look out across the quiet, still valley.

Instantly, from somewhere above him, an immense rock was thrown, narrowly missing his back tire. Pense looked up in amazement to see a black, hairy, manlike figure standing on the butte, arms raised overhead in preparation for throwing another boulder. Frantically the motorcyclist tried to start his engine as the huge projectiles were lobbed with superhuman strength all around him. Pense lost no time in beating a hasty retreat down the side of the ridge, throttle on full. Doubtless, the creature's aim was accurate and he chose to simply warn the rider away, rather than injuring him for the intrusion as he might have. The encounter was reported to Bailey's team and Pense was later to join them in night tracking expeditions. While a healthy fear and respect for the creature's size, strength, and intelligence was instilled in all the men joining the HDSRT, they shared the same compulsive desire to see Bigfoot again.

John Baylor of Lancaster, California, was also to become a member of the group because of an incident occurring to his twelve-year-old son Bret that same year. It was summer. The Baylor residence is on the outskirts of town, at the desert's edge. An alert child with tousled brown hair and sparkling eyes, Bret related the following to investigators:

"My sister Stefanie and I were walking down this dirt road about ten o'clock in the day. We were just talking and looking around. I happened to glance up on Lovejoy Butte and I yelled, 'Guy!' He was looking down at the road and he turned his head and looked at us . . . this huge thing behind the boulder just looking at us! He was brown. I thought it was an ape. The hair around his face was white and his head was kind of pointed. The hair all over his body was brown. We started backing up and then ran about fifteen yards and I had to pick Stef up because she couldn't run fast enough. When we got to the road, I turned around and it was gone!"

Mrs. Joyce Baylor knew by Bret's many stuttering attempts to get the story out through chattering teeth that he had undergone something far out of the ordinary. Little Stefanie, who was younger and shorter, had only glimpsed the creature as a dune had obscured much of her vision, but she was plainly upset by her brother's reactions of terror. The Baylors drove through the deserted buttes seeing only the rocky crags shimmering with heat waves from the broiling midday sun; the dry mesquite bushes dotting the landscape stood unmoving in the hot stillness. Nothing of the size described by Bret could have been hiding behind them. Yet Bigfoot investigators located massive footprints near the high rocks on Lovejoy Butte, where Bret and Stefanie reported they saw the apelike figure.

For some reason, the extraordinary seemed attracted to the area near the Baylor residence, for it had been only a few months prior to this time that the UFO with flashing red, green, and white lights came over their house out of the early darkness, hovering above the telephone pole just beyond the mailbox. It was witnessed by twelve children ranging downward from age sixteen. They thought at first it was lightning illuminating the sky.

The girls were in the Baylor garage, perfecting a drill-team routine for school. The boys were taking practice basketball shots in the driveway. While most of the children ran to the driveway's edge to observe something resembling an iron cable or hose being lowered from the base of the craft to touch the wires, the younger girls, including Stefanie Baylor, stayed within the safety of the lighted garage.

"It looked like two plates put together with a dome on top and no wings!" was one description given.

"And when it stayed still, it just made that high-pitched humming noise. Like, if it had been a helicopter, you could have heard the sound!" was another.

"It was as big as this lot—about a half acre," said Bret's older brother.

For fifteen long, tense, and unreal minutes, the huge craft remained hovering over the wires. Then suddenly, at a high rate of speed, it took off in the direction of the microwave tower on top of a butte to the east, leaving the frightened children staring in awe after it.

Two fantastic anomalies occurring within a few months. A close-encounter UFO sighting and a brown, shaggy Bigfoot seen in the same area. The factor of coincidence? Was it meaningful or grabbing at straws? There had been other coincidences in the Mojave to puzzle both Bigfoot and UFO researchers.

November 1971. Three hunters in the Lucerne Valley began to set up camp just below a ridge when a disk-shaped, brilliantly glowing object described as about the size of a car came over the mountains, hovered for a few moments, and then disappeared. Mystified by the appearance of still another similar UFO, the men climbed to the top of the ridge to get a better view of the valley floor. After some ten minutes of sky watching, a self-luminous, football-shaped object appeared.

"It descended very smoothly to mountaintop level," one of the witnesses stated. "It continued down the contour of the mountainside, across the desert floor, and finally settled on a small plateau. The next thing we knew, *something* got out of the craft and started scanning the area."

Whatever it was began moving rapidly toward the astonished hunters, who ran in the opposite direction toward their camp. Their guns pointed at the top of the ridge, the men waited with pounding hearts. Within seconds, branches were heard cracking, and out of the darkness, two unintelligible cries were uttered. Then it was silent. The hunters spent the night huddled in their sleeping bags, anxiously awaiting daybreak.

In the morning, five round impressions were found in the soil, three of them forming a triangle, the other two close together and ten feet off to one side. The men believe the impressions were made by the saucer when it landed. Its occupant remained a mystery.

Taken from the files of the UFO Research Institute in Redondo Beach, directed by Stanton T. Friedman, nuclear physicist and eminent UFO authority-lecturer, comes the following.

On an evening in 1972, three airmen stationed at George Air Force Base in Victorville (some forty miles east as the crow flies from the Antelope Valley) observed an orange glowing object about the size of the moon but moving low and adjacent to the barracks. As the fiery UFO veered west, in the direction of the desert, the men jumped into their cars and pursued it, speeding down a dusty access road at 50 mph. The object maintained its parallel position to their right, staying just ahead of them. No details were visible within the glowing brilliance emitted from the craft.

After a chase of some ten miles, the object vanished. The airmen slowed their vehicles and looked up. The stationary stars blinked back without signs of any skyward intruder. The men wondered if the craft had landed, turning off its lights.

They walked into the bleak desert toward the area where the object was last sighted, then they froze. A short distance ahead of them stood two cylinders, estimated between nine and ten feet tall, measuring some three feet in diameter. Moonlight reflected off the eerie metallic surfaces. *Nothing* like that should have been in this portion of the desert. There was no construction underway. They ran for their cars, looking back occasionally over their shoulders at the two ominous columns shimmering out of the shadows from Joshua trees.

The following day, the airmen returned, but the metallic objects were gone, as if they never had been there. The hard desert soil gave no indication of trace marks. Investigation by physicist Stan Friedman revealed no further evidence. The witnesses remained adamant in their testimony.

After the winter, from recreational areas in the mountains bordering the Antelope Valley on the south came a rash of reports about a huge, hair-covered, upright-walking creature who left three-toed tracks measuring eighteen inches long. And this being also seemed curious about Ron Bailey.

It was now early 1973. The veteran and his trackers searched for their elusive quarry. They had hiked well into the high desert on this occasion, following up recent sighting reports coming out of the area. As they packed over the side of a tall butte, a deep print was outlined in the glare from Bailey's flashlight, over twelve inches long, narrow, and clearly showing only three toes. The veteran called out for his group to stop and take a look.

"It wasn't made by any animal that I'd ever heard of," Bailey said. "It wasn't human and it wasn't made by someone faking a hoax way out there. The tracks were plain, fresh, and made by something which had passed that way just a few hours before."

Because of the rocky terrain, no further footprints were located that evening, and so, in the early hours of the morning, the men disbanded. Bailey had just climbed into bed beside his sleeping wife when the heavy thumping noise began at the rear of the house they had recently purchased. "It sounded like someone was stomping!" he said.

A neighbor's dog yelped as if someone were beating it, and the thudding sound continued, repeated over and over in a fixed position. Bailey grabbed for his clothes and his gun. It was impossible to see anything from the bedroom window, so Bailey walked outside, just in time to observe a dark figure running away, in the direction of the desert.

"It was a pretty good size, moving at a pretty good pace. Whatever it was, was heading for the hills," the veteran relates. "Margaret and I stayed up the rest of the night, and when morning came, we checked the sage field to the rear of our home. The footprints "were three-toed and well sunk in, like it had deliberately and repeatedly stomped in the same spot."

Obviously the creature wanted Bailey to notice him . . . but why? Is there something in the veteran's background, his military training in jungle tracking, that has developed certain animal awarenesses or instincts such as the mountain men of old possessed? Does Bigfoot sense this, following him to his residence in an effort to communicate? Or could it be that Bailey represents a threat to them?

The veteran disclaims any psychic abilities. He calls it "feeling vibes" and can sense when they are near, even to determining how many of the creatures are hidden in the shadows of the forests or buttes. There is one they have familiarly nicknamed Big Ben, a dark-brown hairy colossus towering some twelve feet in height. He leaves five-toed tracks measuring twenty-four inches with a nine-inch span across the base of the heel. Big Ben's stride exceeds the inconceivable length of twenty feet at a run; the stride at a normal pace is about eight feet. Bailey and his team know. They have tracked him for over a year.

What is even more curious is that the veteran feels Big Ben acknowledges the hunt. The incident in August 1973 is a case in point, and as Bailey came closer to Big Ben's kind, the behemoth doubled back to even the score by terrorizing Bailey's wife, Margaret.

On this particular summer night, the group included John and Joyce Baylor. The ladies remained in one of the cars parked at the base of the mountain trail while the men climbed the steep, narrow canyon. As they gained elevation, they could hear scuffling sounds ahead of them in the darkness.

"Whatever was up there was *big*, and there were more than one of them," Bailey said. "Then the rocks started coming down at us from behind the bushes and trees, thrown at us like we were getting in too close. I was armed. Apparently they didn't like it. Of course, they didn't know it was for my own protection."

The men decided to retreat and began picking their way down the trail on the side of the mountain. It was a dangerous situation. The rocky ledge on which they walked was extremely narrow and still the rocks came at them from above. As one hit at Bailey's right heel, he lost his footing, falling on the seat of his pants. As he scrambled to his feet, he was angry at the entire frustrating situation.

He looked uphill in the direction of the attackers, and the thing he calls the "mind grab" began. "It was happening just like before, this overpowering feeling cutting into my own thoughts and trying to take control," Bailey said. "It wasn't exactly in words—more like a feeling. It was telling me to put down my gun and walk to it."

Almost in a hypnotic state from the telepathic urging, the veteran found himself obeying the command, laying down his gun, and walking slowly up the dark canyon. Then his military disciplines of self-control took over. As he put it, "I grabbed myself *back* to myself and caught what I was doing. At the moment when my mind was released, I was instantly back to being mad again so I picked up some rocks at my feet and started throwing them at the creatures."

A voice from one of the men calling to him broke Bailey's exasperation and he rejoined the team waiting below. Only John Baylor's car remained at the base of the mountain trail. The Bailey car was gone and so were the two women. The peel-out marks from the tires indicated the vast hurry they had left in.

Now concerned, the men drove rapidly out of the canyon toward the Bailey residence. Bailey made radio contact with his wife over the Citizens Band radio, but Margaret wouldn't discuss what had transpired over the channel. Her voice was tense. "Yes, we saw something. I'll tell you about it when you get home."

The attractive brunette met them at the door, more upset and unstrung than her husband had ever seen her. She nervously related the following.

As the men had hiked the upper canyon, the two women sat quietly in the darkened car. Suddenly, from behind the bushes had emerged a gigantic, bulky silhouette that passed slowly in front of the vehicle. Its proportions were out of some nightmare. The young sycamore trees in the area stand at a height between ten and twelve feet. The head of the creature was clearly defined *above* the tops of those trees. It moved with no apparent haste. Across the road, a motor home was parked. "I could see its form outlined by the moonlight against the trailer and it was well head and shoulders over the top of it," Margaret related.

Bailey was convinced the one his wife had seen was none other than Big Ben, and when they returned to the canyon at dawn, the scattered giant footprints made that identification concrete by their very size. But Big Ben hadn't been alone that night as he allowed himself to be seen. Ranging in various sizes near where the cars had been parked were smaller prints, indicating at least two other creatures had been with him.

"They put prints in a lot of places that didn't make any sense," Bailey said. "They were facing all different directions, and then a group of them would trek off into a flat area and then stop completely for no reason. There were footprints helter-skelter all over the place."

Primate playfulness or primal man protecting himself and perhaps not lacking in a sense of fairness? Did the gargantuan know what response the two women would have at the sight of him? Was he just curious about his trackers as they were about seeing Big Ben's kind?

Helter-skelter tracks going nowhere. A victory dance? A war dance? Establishing territorial rights or a laughing fit. Do primates laugh? Why do they want Ron Bailey to meet them face to face?

This particular canyon leads down into the flatlands of the Mojave Desert and terminates in the barren, sandy, and rocky area known as the Buttes. It is a logical route of travel, providing game and water as the snows melt in the high country. The path offers a variety of fruit in the spring and crosses the sweet-smelling alfalfa fields in the lowlands. It is along this route, which essentially runs in a straight line, that the creatures have been consistently sighted. Then late in the autumn, as if affording a last glimpse before moving on to some unknown destination or perhaps returning to the high country to be dormant for the winter, the manlike creatures are seen in the Buttes.

It was here in 1973 that Kent Lacy, formerly a newscaster for Palmdale's Station KUTY (currently with

Station KAFY in Bakersfield), was to experience the most horrifying moments of his life. A close friend of Bailey's, Lacy had joined the research team on another Bigfoot stakeout near a shallow cave where footprints had been found.

During the night, a hair-covered figure was seen moving across the valley, its form outlined against the sandy-colored rocks by the full moon. The character-istic rank odor of the creature had momentarily filled the air. Attempts to follow it proved futile, and near daybreak the trackers disbanded. The newscaster drove alone on the dirt trail out of the desolate Buttes and the sound began—faintly, almost imperceptibly. At first he thought it was the desert wind, rising in pitch as it rushed across the tops of sagebrush and through the Joshua trees.

Then the sound increased in intensity, a plaintive wail much like a woman shrilly moaning in pain. It moved closer and closer to his Baja Buggy until, as Lacy put it, "I thought the thing was almost standing right on top of the car!"

Dawn was still too far away to provide any real light. Lacy raced down the rock-strewn road with head-lights bouncing, the inhuman screams ringing in his ears. A tape recording of the alleged cries of Bigfoot were sent by Stan Gordon, director of the Pennsylvania Center for UFO Research, to southern California in-vestigators, who played them for the Palmdale news-caster. With visible excitement, Lacy identified them as the sounds he had heard.

Were these the same "unintelligible cries" heard by the three hunters camped in the Mojave in 1971, fear-fully watching the UFO occupant coming closer? Is Bigfoot the remnant of an ancient Indian tribe, surviv-ing on highly developed senses and hypnotic tech-niques? If so, will "civilized" man, who has externalized himself into cultural and technological outlets, be any mental match for the creature should a confrontation take place in some remote forest?

There is still another consideration: the coincidence factor of increased UFO sightings and the abrupt appearance of a hairy, manlike being resembling Sasquatch but having only three toes. Is there alien intervention?

Ron Bailey is not decided on Bigfoot's origin or attempts to link the creature to any of the unusual, erratically moving lights seen frequently in the Mojave Desert sky. But the veteran has no doubts of its existence. They have encountered each other often and in some unique manner, exchanged thoughts, vying for who would be the victor of those telepathic battles. Bailey doesn't know why he is being sought out by the Bigfoot. He only knows, "We have our own little personal thing going."

The High Desert Sasquatch Research Team has plans for the capture and confinement of one of the creatures. They discourage curiosity seekers and big-game hunters from joining them in their tracking efforts but will share information with accredited scientific bodies.

7

A Conversation with Bigfoot?

"When I first heard the screams, I thought someone was being murdered. I *wanted* to get up and help that person, but I was too scared!"

The speaker was seventeen-year-old Jim Mangano, a tanned, athletic boy whose appearance reflected time spent in surfing, mountain climbing, and enjoying California's outdoors. His encounter with the Bigfoot creature began on a Saturday in October 1974, when he and six companions backpacked into a campground at the crest of the mountains in the Angeles National Forest. After hiking upward for several miles, they left the trail and crossed down to the stream below, curving its serpentine path through the steep, winding canyons.

The group set up camp for the night, and after a brief meal, they sprawled lazily around the blazing fire, playing guitars and singing in the fast-deepening twilight. It was still too early to go to sleep. Mangano walked upstream alone, to sit quietly on a large rock and contemplate the solitude of the forest. His was no formal, studied meditation but rather a communion or merging with his surroundings. Away from the city, his mind was free and at peace.

After about an hour, the teenager came out of his meditation, but this time something was different, out of the ordinary. There wasn't the same relaxation he normally experienced. "I was like in a blank trance. I couldn't pull myself out of it. I kept waiting . . . for something to enter my mind . . . waiting for *something* which I couldn't figure out," he explained.

As Mangano returned to the campsite, the others were playing a pantomime guessing game. They called to him to join them, but the blond boy sat mutely at the fire's edge, staring past them at nothing.

One of the group, who didn't know the quiet boy as well as the others, questioned, "What's wrong with Jim? Is he on something?"

The rest, knowing Jim's introspective nature, responded that he didn't take drugs, but that being solitary was part of his nature. Abruptly, Mangano arose and, without saying a word, retraced his steps back upstream. One of his closest friends, Val Stemler, explained later, "We knew Jim liked to be by himself sometimes. He liked to listen to things, like sounds of the forest, so when he walked off, we just ignored him."

Subconsciously, the teenager had been "called" back upstream, back to the same rock where he had sat earlier, only he didn't know why or by whom. The mood of the forest and the surroundings now felt "weird." He was growing more frightened by the moment. He believed that this second time he had been gone only fifteen minutes before returning to camp. Val saw him approach out of the shadows and looked at her watch in the light from the fire's embers. It was after eight o'clock. She realized Jim had been gone for two hours.

Now the young people were smoothing the ground and shaking out their bedrolls for the night. "I got into

my sleeping bag, but I was wide awake," Mangano related. "I was trying to figure out what was going on,
wondering why I'd gone back to that rock. Then,
around midnight, I heard the first scream, like a kid
was being murdered out there! It was coming from the
direction where I'd gone upstream.

"I held my breath. Every five seconds it would cry
again. I woke up Lori, who was sleeping next to me,
and she heard it too. There were about five screams in
all and then they stopped. I was horrified inside, like
something was going to happen, and I started to shake.
I *wanted* to get up and go help that person, but I was
really scared to death and thought I'd wait until morning to investigate because I sure didn't want to go looking for him in the dark!"

The other backpackers slept through those five terrifying cries, fatigued by their unaccustomed seven-mile
hike of the day. The girl Mangano had awakened heard
only the final scream and, believing she had dreamed
it, drifted back to sleep. But for the fear-frozen boy, the
night became an endless wait, dreading a repetition of
the strange, high-pitched cries and yet anticipating
them at any moment.

Had he misinterpreted the sounds of normal forest
wildlife? Were the screams the vocalization of coyotes,
the hoots of owls, or the human-sounding wails of
cougars?

In the morning, by the rock upstream where Mangano had twice gone, one giant lean footprint was discovered. Measuring over nineteen inches in length, it
clearly exhibited only three toes. The solitary print was
wedged between two boulders in a sandy spot by the
stream. Whatever had made the huge imprint appeared
to be heading toward the south canyon's almost vertical
wall.

Those were the events reported to the Angeles Sasquatch Association, investigating Bigfoot sightings
throughout southern California. Somewhere in the details were hidden the clues to the mysterious, often
psychical experiences surrounding Bigfoot encounters

which many of the research team had themselves experienced. (See Chapter 5.)

One possibly significant factor often overlooked by Sasquatch researchers was questioned by the ASA. Had any of the girls in the group been menstruating? Yes. Two were. Had this excited a mating urge in the manlike creature or was something else at work to draw him closer to the teenage backpackers? This was a possibility that had to be ruled out, but they suspected something else, something not seen or smelled, but something that Mangano's brain waves sent through the canyons like a transmitter—brain waves, perhaps, not unlike the creature's own.

For with meditation, as with any relaxed mental state or shifting consciousness, comes the Alpha Brain Wave rhythm, running eight to thirteen cycles per second as opposed to the more rapid Beta Brain Waves, which run thirteen to twenty-six cycles per second. The latter waves are linked to anxiety, concerns, and mental concentration. The Alpha breeds inner unity with the surroundings and new perceptions. It is believed that the Alpha can increase hypnotic suggestibility.[1]

Was it a telepathic-hypnotic summons that called Jim Mangano back to that rock upstream—and if so, why? Did the creature feel he could communicate with this boy, who was more oriented to the pulse of nature? But what triggered the time lapse of some hundred minutes in his memory? Was this a by-product of his meditation, wherein the hours lost their meaning? Had Bigfoot hypnotized the boy into forgetting or had Mangano seen something he *wanted* to forget?

Some of the answers to the many questions raised by the Angeles Sasquatch Association lay a short distance in the future, in a dramatic experiment conducted by their consultants, but first the research group wanted to determine if the encounter could be repeated. Mangano was used as bait, and although there were two women in the follow-up group, the factor of a monthly cycle was this time ruled out.

On November 16, 1974, three ASA trackers, Val

Stemler, and Jim Mangano backpacked into the same region of the Angeles National Forest. A level site near the stream was selected to set up camp, a place several miles from the initial episode. Bedrolls were placed away from the steep canyon walls to avoid the danger of rockslides.

Tape recorders, flashlights, and cameras loaded with infrared film were in readiness as gloom settled in the canyons. Of one thing the trackers were certain—trails leading into this area would not be traveled at night by any moonlight hikers. The paths were far too narrow and treacherous to permit any foot traffic after sundown. A misplaced step would result in a fall of several thousand feet.

Winter darkness came upon them rapidly. Jim Mangano was requested to meditate a short distance from the fire, near a thicket of brush and trees. The group spoke in hushed voices so as not to disturb him. Occasionally they would glance at the teenager sitting with his back against a log, eyes closed, After thirty minutes, Mangano got to his feet and began walking slowly, almost somnambulistically, toward the dark rock outcropping downstream. Immediately two of the trackers were at his side.

"They . . . they want me to come to them," the blond boy said in a halting voice, now aware of the sudden activity around him.

It had been determined earlier by the researchers that under no circumstances was Mangano to get out of their sight. "We're going with you," was the response.

The teenager pondered this for a moment, his somewhat dazed eyes staring at some point out in the darkness, his attitude one of listening. "No," he answered softly. "They want me to come alone."

The request was impossible. The creature's intentions toward the boy were unknown. While Mangano warmed himself by the fire, Richard Engels and Neil Forn made their way downstream toward the rock outcropping. The forest was still, seemingly empty. No trace of Bigfoot was found.

About 11:00 P.M., the researchers climbed into their

bedrolls. Strangely fatigued by his meditation, Mangano was already asleep. The first scream cut through the silent fabric of the night like a machete. It was like the trumpet of a bull elephant issuing a mighty challenge, an angry bellow that reverberated through the canyons at a volume more powerful than human capacity. Instantly the group was awake, alert, and braced for the next inhuman sound. It came before tape recorders could be reached. Then an ominous silence settled through the forest. Even the owls had stopped their rhythmic hooting.

The trackers wondered if the creature was angry because they'd prevented a confrontation between itself and Mangano, if indeed that had been in the night's offing. They hadn't long to wait for the answer. Soon, a bulky "something" crashed through the brush on the steep ridge across stream, remaining concealed in the dense thicket and pines.

Shortly before midnight, a barrage of rocks began, missiles not dislodged from the cliff behind them but thrown in a trajectory, narrowly missing the unprotected heads of the campers. It was diabolically timed. As sleep began to overcome the group, the creature would throw still another rock, coming within scant yards of their heads. Some came dangerously closer. Measuring from two to four inches, the rocks were no great threat, yet they could prove fatal upon impact due to the elevation from which they were thrown.

Throughout the long night, the trackers cursed the fact that they hadn't brought hard hats, and then, as another rock could be heard rushing down through pine boughs from above, they generally cursed some more. For what seemed an endless wait until dawn, fury—although impotent—was a better companion than fear.

The difficulties surrounding the investigation of the Bigfoot have a counterpart in still another phenomenon currently under scientific scrutiny—that of the Unidentified Flying Object (UFO). Lacking a "body" to dissect or propulsion unit to examine, researchers must try to reconstruct one from multiwitness accounts and the physical evidence supporting the existence of UFOs.

In the case for the UFO, there are landing traces, altered soil and vegetation, mechanical and physiological effects, as well as photographs and taped sounds. In the case for Bigfoot, there are also photographs and taped vocalizations as well as hair samples, feces, and footprints.

Early in 1964, the work of psychiatrist Dr. Benjamin Simon inadvertently opened a significant gateway for further knowledge. A New Hampshire couple, Barney and Betty Hill, had consulted him because of recurrent nightmares suffered since September 1961. "They were constantly haunted by a nagging anxiety centering around this period of several hours, a feeling that something had occurred—but what?" the psychiatrist stated.[2]

To unlock that door to the amnesia of several hours present in both their minds, Dr. Simon chose hypnotic regression as his tool for therapy. He wasn't prepared for the bizarre data that emerged. He expected to locate some childhood basis for their mutual fears, but he was told that they believed they were taken on board an alien spacecraft and subjected to a series of physical tests. They said the extraterrestrials released them with a posthypnotic suggestion that they would not remember the kidnapping.

Since that pioneering discovery, other professional men have used hypnotic techniques and truth serums with some success in retrieving information from the minds of other time-lapse UFO contactees.[3]

In the case of Jim Mangano, three factors indicated he had undergone something unordinary: his first meditation produced what he called "a blank trance"; there was a compulsion to return to the rock resulting in amnesia of one hour and forty-five minutes; and on the second backpacking trip, there appeared to be some kind of telepathic interplay with the creatures. The circumstances favored hypnotic regression, and the teenager agreed to being taken back to that point in time where his conscious memory was a blank.

The session took place on January 15, 1975, in the Palos Verdes offices of Dr. Robert Jordan. The tall psychiatrist's manner was composed; a warm smile played behind a salt-and-pepper full beard. The doctor had selected hypnotist Donna Welke, director of the School of Applied Hypnosis, a pert, dynamic, and extremely outgoing woman. Jim Mangano liked them both on sight. It was a good start—and the birth of the startling. For, although the ASA researchers had a standard running gag about conquering their fears should the Big Fella ever decide to put a hairy paw on someone's shoulder, no one present in Dr. Jordan's office that day could have anticipated this was one of the things that had occurred, locked in the teenager's memory.

The following is edited from that hypnotic taped session. The psychiatrist had already spoken with Mangano at some length, determining his method of meditation, inquiring about his feeling as to recovering the lost memory and general questions regarding his background. Then Donna Welke took over, explaining to the boy that she would put him into a state of relaxation and he would relate to her the things he saw as if they were unfolding on a theater screen. Thus, whatever frightening or traumatic events occurred, Mangano would not be emotionally involved with them.

She maneuvered her questions superbly, drawing the teenager into the past. He seemed initially hesitant to speak. The hypnotist projected herself into his memory, placing herself on the scene, asking him to join her at the rock. . . .

Donna: Take me with you. Go mentally, just as you would if you were meditating, but stay in contact with me because I am your friend. You said you can meet friends in meditation and I'm into meditation. I can go. I can meet you there. Would you take me with you?

(Jim is on the couch with eyes closed, arms relaxed and folded across his chest. He nods in the affirmative.)

Donna: O.K., then, let's go together. I'm holding your hand . . . tell me when you're there.

(Jim is silent.)

Donna: It's so easy to do. Why are we being kept out of this memory? Let's go! You're free. I'm sitting on that rock, waiting for you. Are you there yet?

Jim: Yes. (His voice is very soft.)

Donna: Very good. You have a lovely spot here, I do agree. It would be very easy to meditate here. How do I get into this meditation, now that I'm sitting on this rock with you?

Jim: Be free.

Donna: O.K., I'm letting myself go. I'm free now. Are you free?

Jim: Yes.

Donna: Good. Now we're free. Our minds are together and we're free to meditate. Is there anyone else around us? Anything else around us?

Jim: Yes.

Donna: What is it? We're not frightened by it because we're here together. Nothing can frighten us. What is it? How can we describe it?

Jim: It . . . it's big!

Donna: It is very big, I agree. What's it saying?

Jim: It's not saying anything.

Donna: I thought it might be trying to communicate.

Jim: It's just looking at us.

Donna: How tall would you say it is?

Jim: I can't see all of it, just the top from the middle up. I'm looking up at it.

Donna: What do you think he thinks of us? Does he think we're silly, sitting on a rock like this? What are your inner feelings?

(Jim is silent.)

Donna: It's a strange thing, but then we've seen strange things before. Help me understand what's going on. Is this being telling us not to remember any of our communication after we come out of our meditation? Maybe there's nothing to see. . . . Is that all he did, just come up and look at us and walk away?

Jim: (His breathing is heavy, rhythmic. He is now deep under hypnosis.) He put his hand on my shoulder.

Donna: Did it feel comfortable?

Jim: Strong!

Donna: O.K., was it warm or cold?

Jim: Warm. (He was later to describe it as "powerful.")

Donna: Very good. Is he mute or are there any words being spoken?

Jim: He's welcoming me.

Donna: How does he do that? Does he say something or is this just a thought he gives you? How do you know?

Jim: (Interrupts) His eyes!

Donna: His eyes tell you. Are these eyes soft or sparkling? Are they eyes you enjoy looking into?

Jim: Uh huh (affirmative).

Donna: O.K., he speaks with his eyes and you know. Does he frighten you in any way?

Jim: He startled me.

Donna: Does he give you any indication that he would like to communicate with you again?

(Jim is silent.)

Donna: Was it just a one-shot thing where you just happened along, because you were in a receptive state of mind or did he call you to this rock?

Jim: He called me . . . with his mind.

Donna: Why?

Jim: To . . . to help him to get out.

Donna: Why does he need to get out?

Jim: (He looks extremely sad, as if about to cry.) The hunters . . . people keep him in.

Donna: How can you help? What does he think you can do? Does he tell you why and give you a purpose?

(Jim is silent.)

Donna: What rules him then? Do other people rule him? Ask him.

Jim: There is a leader. . . .

Donna: He has a leader then. Where is this leader? Will he give you that information?

Jim: No, won't tell me.

Donna: Why? We'll share information with him, our knowledge of our God and our leaders. If he's asking you for help and friendship, then friendship should be equal and shared. Will he share with you?

Jim: Yes, he'll share . . . fruit. (Now he grows visibly excited, half-sitting up with his eyes still closed.) Wait! There's a bunch of them standing, looking down on me. I must be sitting on the ground.

Donna: Can you see the area? Do you know what area you're in?

Jim: No, it's dark. They're saying to tell people . . . tell people they were here first!

Donna: They were here before we were?

Jim: Yes!

Donna: What else?

Jim: They said we're ruining their planet.

Unfortunately, the allotted time was running out and Dr. Jordan's next appointment was waiting in the outer office. The hypnotist began slowly talking the teenager back to the present, giving him the suggestion that he would awake feeling refreshed, with a clear, sharp mind. There was time only for a few subsequent questions directed to Mangano concerning the creatures and their communication. He responded, "They were dark brown. Their eyes were friendly, kind of sad. I never saw their mouths move. He's an intelligent being."

Had this happened in the physical or had Bigfoot projected his thoughts telepathically into a receptive state of mind?

"Jim felt the physical," Donna Welke explained. "He seemed to be able to tell you temperature and feeling and strength and all that. So whether it was happening for real or not, Jim felt it was."

It was what Dr. Simon had tried to clarify after regressing Barney and Betty Hill: "The charisma of hypnosis has tended to foster the belief that hypnosis is the magical and royal road to Truth. In one sense this is so, but it must be understood that hypnosis is a pathway to the truth as it is felt and understood by the patient. The truth is what he believes to be the truth and this may or may not be consonant with the ultimate nonpersonal truth. Most frequently it is."

This possible first breakthrough of communication

between the Bigfoot creature and man got no further than that first hypnotic regression session, for Jim Mangano declined any subsequent meetings. He said it was "too much of a hassle."

In view of the considerable distance for him to travel to Dr. Jordan's office, as well as the time taken somewhere between school, work, and recreational time spent outdoors, this may have been a valid excuse for a busy young man. Yet, why did Mangano later confide to a friend that since the first attempt to unlock the time lapse, he had felt massive, dark shapes moving around outside his home at night, probing his mind? He wasn't sure. He thought he might have been dreaming it.

The message, however partial, had been retrieved out of his memory. It spoke of days past that the Indians tell of, when men and animals walked and talked together. Was it because of his deep respect for nature that Jim Mangano, through meditation, had simply glimpsed that time of long ago?

The evidence supports the fact that his "meeting" was far less mystical, that the manlike creature had been there physically, had placed his hand on the shoulder of a friend, and had spoken of a world now drastically altered for them . . . a world that has forced them into hiding . . . a world that once was theirs.

Perhaps this world may again belong to them if what Odette Tchernine postulates in her book *In Pursuit of the Abominable Snowman* is really a prediction of a future close at hand.

She writes,

I may be verbally flayed for what I am about to say but perhaps after all we are not meant to discover the whole truth about the Snowman, Yeti, Almas or Hairy Man. Perhaps these are the primal rough and secret stock preserved to withstand and survive any final disaster, preserved and hidden as the raw material for a fresh start in evolution should we finally blow up our so-called civilization. There is more to all living humanity than flesh and bones and potential "spare parts." The

Spirit that always walked on the face of the waters remains.

NOTES

1. Jodi Lawrence, *Alpha Brain Waves* (New York, Avon Books, 1972).
2. John G. Fuller, *The Interrupted Journey* (New York, Dell Publishing, 1967).
3. Patrolman Herbert Schirmer, hypnotized by Dr. R. Leo Sprinkle: Condon and Gillmor, *Scientific Study of Unidentified Flying Objects* (New York, Bantam Books, 1969); Charles Hickson and Calvin Parker, hypnotized by Dr. James Harder: Friedman and Slate, "The Truth Behind the Amazing Pascagoula Contact," *SAGA UFO Report* (Spring 1974); Dionisio Llanca, hypnotized by Drs. Santos and Mata: Randle, "The UFO Kidnapping That Challenged Science," *SAGA UFO Report* (Spring 1975).

8

UFO Bigfoot Creatures: The Pennsylvania Effect

The huge glowing ball descended from the sky and slowly came to rest on the hilltop. Fifteen persons in the rural Pennsylvania area claim to have seen it. Three of them, a twenty-two-year-old man and two neighbor boys, ten-year-old twins, boldly approached the object for a closer look. They drove a truck from a nearby farmhouse to the base of the hill. When the headlights of the vehicle dimmed inexplicably, they parked the truck and proceeded on foot.

Near the top of the hill, at a distance of about 250 feet, they stopped in awe to observe the brilliant phenomenon. It was rather dome-shaped from where they stood and it appeared to be about one hundred feet in diameter at its base. It emitted a noise like a revved-up rotary lawn mower.

Suddenly they heard what they thought were screams,

and one of the twins yelled out that there was something moving along a fence line that bordered a pasture to one side. The rail fence was about seventy-five feet away. As the other twin and the man turned to look, two figures emerged from the shadows in the illumination cast by the UFO. The sight of them was terrifying. They were hair-covered and apelike, only they were very tall and had large yellowish-green eyes that seemed to glow; and they were making babylike crying noises.

The first boy had seen enough and bolted for the truck downhill. The other boy and the young man, who carried a 30/06 rifle, momentarily stood their ground. The rifle was loaded with tracer ammunition. The man raised the rifle and fired several times over the creatures' heads. When they kept coming, he then fired directly at one of them, apparently hitting it. It reeled slightly, made a whining sound, and raised a long hairy arm as if to warn its companion.

At the same instant, the UFO suddenly disappeared —vanished, as if it had never been there, except for a low-lying luminescence that lingered at the site.

The man and the boy at this point decided they had seen enough, as well, and turned heel.

Hogwash or a Hollywood scriptwriter's imagining? Neither. It happened something like this at about 9 P.M. October 25, 1973, near Uniontown, Pennsylvania. The incident was investigated by state police, the Pennsylvania Center for UFO Research,[1] and Dr. Berthold Eric Schwarz, a psychiatrist who interviewed the man, the boys, their families, the witnesses to the aerial phenomenon, and others involved.[2] What made it unique among myriad other UFO incidents that swept Pennsylvania that year was the coincidence of the creatures' appearance. There had been many reports throughout the state of hairy apelike creatures seen where UFO activity had been reported. The UFO Center alone logged more than one hundred creature reports. But the Uniontown case was the first multiple-witness report tying the two phenomena together. For Stan Gordon, director of the UFO Center, it was also the first occasion where he would witness one of the weird UFO-creature incidents in progress.

At 9:45 P.M., a state trooper arrived at the scene and proceeded up the hill with Stephen, as we'll call the young man. Where the UFO had come to rest, the officer noted that in a circular area about 150 feet in diameter there was enough illumination just above ground level to read a newspaper by. He also noted that, when they moved to the fence line and then along the outer edge of the woods at the upper end of the pasture, something large concealed in the trees moved with them.

At 1:30 A.M., a UFO Center team—comprising Stan Gordon, founder of the study group and owner of a local electronic firm; a retired Air Force pilot; a Civil Defense radiation technician; a sociology student; and a professional photographer—arrived and were taken to the hilltop. For thirty minutes the men searched, inspected, and tested the area for evidences and signs without success. The illumination was gone. No unusual footprints or marks on the ground could be found. There was no blood trail suggesting an injured creature. There was no unusual radiation.

It might have ended there, but as the group prepared to leave, a bull pastured on the slope suddenly became restless as if disturbed by something in the wooded area uphill. At, the same time, Stephen's German shepherd, which had tagged along, became intent on the tree line.

The party decided to further investigate when, suddenly, Stephen stopped and began, rubbing his face and eyes. George Lutz, the retired pilot, asked him if he was O.K. The six-foot-two-inch-tall, 250-pound man didn't reply but began to quiver and shake. He began breathing heavily, finally growling like a beast.

In the next moment, with his face contorted and animallike, Stephen seized his own father, who'd been walking with the group, and threw him to the ground. He also knocked Lutz down. Then, while the others watched in astonishment, he went lurching off across the pasture, swinging his arms wildly, snarling and shrieking in a voice no one recognized as his own.

The German shepherd at first turned on its master, rushing Stephen as if to attack when he knocked down his elderly father, but then it backed off and cowered, whimpering uncontrollably.

In another moment, Dennis Smeltzer, a member of Gordon's group, complained of feeling light-headed and sank to his knees. David Smith and David Baker, the Civil Defense technician and the photographer, went to his side, where almost immediately they experienced the same effect compounded by difficulty in breathing. A choking, sulfurous odor had filled the air, according to Gordon, who was also affected.

In the pasture, Stephen suddenly collapsed facedown in a grassy area covered with cow dung. His father and Lutz caught up with him there, and with the help of each other, all of the party began to retreat off the hill.

Gordon had tape-recorded most of the incident. He later said that Stephen's behavior had been animallike and too extraordinary not to have been authentic. "The sound that fellow made, it couldn't have been made by a human trying to make it—there is no way words can describe what happened there."

As the incident further developed, Stephen would fall into a trancelike state and blurt out prophecies of doom. Had he been possessed by the creatures, by the UFO intelligence perhaps behind them? What did the seizure and the effects dealt the state trooper and other investigators mean?

On the night of February 6, 1974, again in Uniontown, a woman we'll call Thelma Arnold thought she heard tin cans rattling at her front door. Thinking that dogs were upsetting the garbage, she got up from where she sat watching television, retrieved a loaded sixteen-gauge shotgun kept in a handy location, and stepped out the door to frighten the dogs away.

What she saw in the porch light only a few feet away hardly fit the description of dogs, however; it was rather a tall, hair-covered apelike creature, which immediately raised both hands above its head as in a gesture of surrender. It was a horrible shock for Thelma. There was no time to think the matter through. She pointed the shotgun at the creature's gut and fired.

If the story ended there, it would be unusual enough, and pathologists would have had a fine time trying to piece together the mangled viscera and entrails of the remarkable beast. But Thelma apparently had blasted the creature right out of sight, for there was nothing left where it had been except the smoking snout of the shotgun barrel.

"It just disappeared in a flash of light," she told investigators.

The incident was coupled with later reports of hairy giants prowling the wooded area, and indeed, it had been preceded by a year-long wave of UFO-creature activity throughout Pennsylvania and adjoining states. Was it mere hysteria or hallucination? Or, as it would more credibly seem in the case of the dome-shaped UFO that disappeared when Stephen fired his rifle, was the creature quite real and a more mysterious force at play?

In California and throughout the Pacific Northwest, for more than a hundred years people have reported sightings of Bigfoot. Each year there are more and more reports of sightings and footprints found, sightings and footprints that bear striking resemblance to those associated in Pennsylvania and elsewhere with the UFO creatures. Are the two creatures one and the same? What were they now doing in Pennsylvania? And Sykesville, Maryland?

In May 1973, at Sykesville, a UFO with flashing red lights reportedly descended over a reservoir and dropped a large object before flitting off into other dimensions. The next day and for two weeks afterward, local police were plagued with reports that an eight-foot-tall monster with big luminous eyes was prowling the countryside. It was another of the few cases on record where a Bigfootlike creature appeared in direct conjunction with a UFO visit. It was investigated at length by Dr. Theodore Roth, assistant director of the Baltimore Zoo.

"Some of the reports we had were from fairly good witnesses who allegedly shot at the thing at a range closer than twenty feet, and there was no reaction other than the thing disappearing right in front of them," Roth said.

In British Columbia, a Skagit River Indian legend[3] tells of a Bigfoot tribe whose individuals developed a mental ability to delude themselves and others at will that they could make themselves invisible. Is it possible that the legend alludes to the UFO creatures and that they've been with us all along?

In his book *The Uninvited Visitors*,[4] the late zoologist Ivan Sanderson suggests that creatures such as Bigfoot in America, the Yeti of the Himalayas, the Alma of Siberia, and like creatures reported the world over might be UFO-related and, indeed, might possess the ability to become invisible, "either intrinsically, or by influencing the observer, as in hypnosis."

The relatively recent development and use of atomic energy might account for the onslaught of UFO-creature sightings and events, Sanderson speculates. He says that perhaps the "more competent types" behind the UFOs and the creatures were caught unawares by human progress and were forced into a crash program of Earth surveillance and that of man's activity affecting the Earth: ". . . they seem to have stumbled and bumbled around just as we are doing with our so-called space program, with blowups, crash-landings, vaporizations and all the rest. . . .

"What is more, they seem to have resorted to what I call 'Laikas' [name of a dog orbited in space by the USSR early in space-flight experiments] in the form of these 'hairy giants' which look exactly like some of our own hairy primitives, don't wear clothes, leave naked humanoid foot-tracks, and behave generally just like trained chimpanzees. . . ."

Wherever the creature phenomenon has been reported (consider included Big Ben of the Mojave Desert, Momo of Missouri, and the Skunkman of the Everglades), the creatures have a proclivity for rapid disappearance from the face of human reality. Evidence is seldom found except for an occasional handful of hair and the enormous footprints. Yet the creatures are seen, and they do seem to have an effect on human nature whether caught in the act or not.

Gordon cites an incident where a man was standing alone in his bathroom late at night, shaving in front of a mirror over a washbasin. The bathroom window next to him at shoulder level was open. Suddenly a foul odor filled the air and he began sneezing. He turned to the open window and found himself looking directly into two large eyes glowing red and the hideous face of a hairy monster.

In his fright, he slammed the window shut, knocked over several jars on the sink, and ran gasping to the living room to tell his family. Members of the family immediately were concerned about a heart condition he suffered, but they also smelled the foul odor in the air. There were no further incidents that night, but in the morning the man had a heart seizure and was hospitalized.

Hysteria, hallucination, or the real thing and a heart-attack consequence?

Gordon investigated: "The location was Rhodabaugh Road, just off Route 30 parallel to the Greengate Mall shopping complex [Greensburg, Pennsylvania]. The area is densely wooded and there are streams, caves, and mine shafts throughout the immediate vicinity.

"I interviewed the man and found out that his fourteen-year-old son had, in the company of several other boys, seen some kind of creature about a month before. I talked with the boys, who all seemed very serious and told the same story separately."

The boys had hiked through the woods across from their homes toward Greengate Mall. Along the way they heard noises in the thickets ahead and one of them threw a rock in that direction. They'd imagined it was a deer, but from the opposite side of the thicket, an enormous gorillalike figure emerged, walking on two legs. As they watched, it proceeded to cross Rhodabaugh Road and disappear into a wooded area behind the heart-attack victim's house.

Gordon searched both wooded areas. To his amazement, behind the victim's house he discovered a large, bare footprint, which he subsequently photographed and cast.

"The footprint measured thirteen inches long and eight inches wide," he said. "The bone structure was quite visible in the great toe, and what looked like protruding bones or muscles could also be seen."

Though he found no other prints or physical evidence, he felt that the man, the man's family, and the boys were sincere and that the footprint was authentic.

Later the same day he investigated a similar story in a nearby area, where a man claimed that a creature with glowing red eyes had watched him through a window of his home. In this instance, police had found an eighteen-inch-long footprint in the yard. The chief difference seemed to be that this man had a stout heart and suffered no ill consequences except a good case of the chills.

Had the creatures meant to appear before these people or were their appearances simply the "bumbling" effect described by Sanderson, with the heart attack an inadvertent consequence?

As word of the incidents spread, so did a near-panic through Westmoreland County, according to Gordon. Police switchboards were jammed, the UFO Center's switchboard took hundreds of phone calls. "Some calls were from people who claimed to have seen such creatures in the past but were afraid to talk about it," Gordon said. "Others wanted to know how they could protect themselves." Armed vigilantes were out. Back roads in the wooded areas were bumper to bumper with sightseers looking for Bigfoot.

But the big-eyed giant who liked to look but not be seen for the most part remained as fleeting as a taxpayer's dollar, and about as difficult to account for, according to Gordon's reports.

In Derry, on August 21, 1973, a woman was awakened about 2:30 A.M. by a feeling that she was being watched. It was a warm night. She'd gone to bed with the window open and the drapes drawn. She turned to look out through the drapes and found herself face to face with a monster. The drapes had been parted. The windowsill was nine feet above ground level. The thing was right there, looking at her from less than three feet away.

Paralyzed with fright, she simply lay there. The creature's eyes were upright and oval, and dark with no whites, and no eyelids or eyelashes, apparently. The nose was pushed in, and under the eyes the skin appeared burned and like a patch. It did nothing until she moved involuntarily, then, very awkwardly it seemed, the face retreated, moving straight back and away from the window. Outside, everything was quiet, she recalled, yet she could hear no movement made by the creature.

She had not yet built up courage enough to move or yell for help when her fourteen-year-old daughter suddenly burst into the bedroom, crying that she'd been awakened by something and had just seen a huge shadow across her bedroom wall.

Gordon said a police chief had contacted the UFO Center about the incident. The police chief said he knew the woman and her daughter and felt they were sincere. They'd phoned the police only after hearing a rumor about a creature being shot, saying they wanted to know if it was the same thing that had appeared at their windows. They claimed that for two days an odor of rotten meat had lingered in and about the house. From all indications it seemed clear that whatever had skulked about their home was no ordinary Peeping Tom.

Three days later a seven-foot-tall apelike creature was reportedly seen in nearby Herminie, in this instance at dusk. A man said he'd sat down to rest after mowing his lawn when his dog, chained in the backyard, began barking excitedly. When he went to investigate, he found the dog, frantically trying to break free, and about thirty feet beyond him, the creature, standing motionless at the foot of the yard. He immediately ran into the house to get a gun, he said, but when he returned, the creature had disappeared. In the yard, a freshly broken branch was found under a tree and a footprint eighteen inches long and seven inches wide. As in other cases, there was a strong, foul odor in the air.

In similar reports:

—A woman and her son heard scratching on their trailer home and what sounded like a baby crying. They opened the door to confront a huge apelike figure that ran and disappeared with their screams.

—A young woman visiting a cemetery in the early evening was horrified to see a large apelike creature suddenly step out of the nearby trees and approach her child, who'd wandered off. She ran, grabbed up the baby, fled to her car, and drove away. She'd smelled a stench like rotten eggs.

—A man and his wife was awakened by a banging outside their home. They looked out a window to see an eight-foot-tall hair-covered creature with its back to them, standing in their drive, apparently peering into a window of the house next door, where several children were sleeping. As they phoned the police, almost simultaneously a neighbor three doors away was also phoning the police to report a creature sighting.

In all, through 1973, including thhe multiple-witness Uniontown incident linking creatures with UFOs, the Pennsylvania Center for UFO Research documented more than one hundred Bigfoot sightings that seemed to have credible bases in fact. Many if not most were like the foregoing, pointing toward a gigantic apelike creature with a penchant for looking in on individuals in a private or isolated setting and an acute dislike for being discovered in the act. Hundreds of other sightings and incidents were reported, according to Gordon, but were discounted as hoaxes, hysteria, and mistaken identity. This was in Pennsylvania alone, during a year when UFO-creature activity was rampant throughout the United States.

Despite the lack of evidence of direct physical harm to humans, and though it would seem that the creatures bore no ill will per se, their mere appearance in conjunction with UFO activity nevertheless spread shock and alarm through segments of the human community, in some cases with serious consequence to individual lives.

When Stephen went berserk in Gordon's presence, growling and carrying on like a wild animal, his father and some of the others present felt the creatures had "possessed" him. Dr. Berthold Eric Schwarz psychiatrically examined the young man after the incident and interviewed most of the principals involved. "A study of his past life revealed no evidence of any previous similar dissociative, disorientated behaviour, nor any character traits like sleepwalking, sleep talking, fainting, amnesia, trancelike states, etc. Furthermore, there is no past history for convulsive disorder, brain injury, or disease, that could cause temporal lobe seizure or automatism analogues to Stephen's reaction to the creatures. The information derived from Stephen, his parents, neighbours and several physicians indicates that the [seizure] was a specific reaction to the UFO-creatures experience—a solitary, outstanding event in Stephen's life."

Stephen's behavior could have been self-induced, Dr. Schwarz explains, but it might not have been. "There is an element of psi in many UFO sightings. Stephen's experience has so many bizarre aspects . . . that one wonders if the common force was a UFO-induced psi-effect, and if this influence could in some way, either independently or in conjunction with the psychopathology, have effected the changes in Stephen and accounted for his [seizure]. Could the UFO and the creatures have materialized or dematerialized into another dimension? How does one prove this? What explanations are there? If materialization were possible, then this could account for many strange happenings and it would not be unusual to anticipate many wild and unheard-of science-fiction-like yet 'real' effects."

Possessed or not, Stephen had undergone a change in personality that would have lasting effect. Whether the UFO and the creatures were "neighbors" of ours in another space-time dimension, as UFO book-author Brad Steiger has theorized and as Dr. Schwarz in the

Uniontown case found cause to wonder, their influence and *potential* for influencing human life seems obvious.

Dr Schwarz concludes that Stephen's strange behavior and prophecies of mankind's destruction (he doubted that the United States would realize its bicentennial unless man "straightened up," according to Schwarz) probably resulted from past emotional experiences (*i.e.*, a painful relationship with an authoritarian father) combined with the horror of the moment. Yet he adds: "But who knows? . . . Suffice it to say that this case demonstrates (1) here-and-now implicit danger to those witnesses who are involved in such an experience, (2) perhaps more so, the dangers to those who study such people, (3) the challenging need for collateral, psychiatric investigations, and (4) the urgent need for a bold but responsible stance in finding out all we can about the UFO-creature relationship."

In California and throughout the Pacific Northwest, Bigfoot creatures are nearly universal in Indian legend, despite the wide diversity of physical, cultural, and geographical differences between tribal groups there. Historically, footprints and sightings—even a capture of a juvenile—have been recorded and reported ever since the time of Lewis and Clark. None other than Theodore Roosevelt wrote a stirring account of two trappers and their encounters with a crazed Bigfoot, which eventually killed one of the trappers. In recent years, notably since the late 1940s after the first atomic-bomb tests were conducted and mass destruction was wrought by the United States in Japan, Bigfoot incidents have become almost commonplace, numbering in the hundreds each year. While UFO activity is seldom reported as part of the phenomenon on the West Coast, and Bigfoot there is seldom accused of prophesying through the mouths of those who encounter him, is it possible that he is, and always has been, a tool of the "more competent types," the UFO-intelligences? Have we been witnessing, simply, his deployment to other geographical bases in the nation? Is he a higher intelligence's answer to our military reservist?

The Skagit River Indian legend either does or does

not have some basis in fact. If it does, perhaps there is a close UFO-creature relationship; and perhaps, as the Uniontown case and many others like it across the country suggest, the Bigfoot creatures can make themselves invisible, and can be made invisible, through mind control or delusion of others who might find their presence objectionable or threatening. One does not have to look far in Indian legend or modern-day report to find references to the great creature's mental embrace, or, indeed, situations that, except for a lack of obvious "contactee" message, parallel UFO-related Bigfoot encounters outside the Pacific Northwest. Stephen's vague "warning" to mankind may simply mean that the creatures have been called into action; it may have been a precursor of more specific warnings to come.

In point of fact, could Bigfoot exist *anywhere* and stay beyond the reach of human curiosity and alarm without great mental ability and power over the human mind? Stan Gordon, in his assessment of the Uniontown incident and others of the continuing Pennsylvania UFO-creature flap, argues that the Bigfoot of West Coast tradition and the Pennsylvania variety could not be one and the same, chiefly, it seems, because the former usually has five toes and the latter only three. Three-toed (and four-toed) creatures have been reported out West, in fact, and descriptions otherwise are usually much the same. "Perhaps if they're constructing and deconstructing and reconstructing themselves, they forgot to put on the rest of the toes!" as Dr. Roth of the Baltimore Zoo equipped.

NOTES

1. Stan Gordon, "UFOs, In Relation To Creature Sightings in Pennsylvania," MUFON UFO Symposium (1974). (Gordon founded and now directs the Pennsylvania Center for UFO Research in Greensburg, Pennsylvania. The center's staff is

comprised of volunteers from fields of science, medicine, engineering, education, and law enforcement. The organization's stated purpose is to investigate UFO phenomena and disseminate information regarding its findings. It takes no stand on the origin, makeup, or purpose of UFOs and UFO-related phenomena.)

2. Berthold Eric Schwarz, "Berserk: A UFO-Creature Encounter," *Flying Saucer Review* (Vol. 20, No. 1, 1974).

3. Emerson N. Matson, *Legends of the Great Chiefs* (New York, Thomas Nelson, Inc., 1972).

4. Ivan T. Sanderson, *The Uninvited Visitors* (New York, Cowles, 1967).

9

What Do You Do About a Monster?

In the summer of 1975, in widely separated areas across the United States, two new names for the hairy, manlike being emerged: the Noxie Monster and the Foothill Monster. They varied only in size—one seven feet tall and the other a whopping ten feet tall, according to eyewitness accounts. And although one was in Oklahoma and the other in California, law-enforcement officials in both states shared similar anxieties. Not about the monster. About the monster-hunters.

"A bunch of idiots running around drinking beer and carrying rifles and CB radios!" Nowata County Sheriff Bob Arnold said from Oklahoma.[1]

And from a police officer in Corona, California: "I tell you, somebody will get shot if people don't stay away from up there!"[2]

Noxie is a small farming community with rolling,

timber-covered hills on the Oklahoma-Kansas border. Their monster was estimated at seven feet with a man-like face, completely hair-covered and having glowing red eyes. Two men claim to have shot at it with no results.

"It just walked away."

Sheriff Arnold couldn't discover where "Ol' Noxious," as he called him, had walked to. The grass was not flattened down along its reported path. In fact, the Sheriff could hardly *get* to the path as he found himself mobbed by reporters, sightseers, and gun-toting townsfolk. There was only one way to break it up.

"We issued an ultimatum in three newspapers, over two radio stations, and person to person that anyone found in the area with a gun was going to jail." He also told reporters to stay away because they might get shot; he said he'd hate to have to fill up his jail with "some of the good people around here."

Sheriff Arnold didn't think it was a hoax, that someone was walking around in a fur-covered costume. "Not in that area, not even in broad daylight. Those people up there protect themselves as best they can and are liable to plink at anything."

But he did think the frightened witnesses had misinterpreted whatever it was they saw, especially when he could find no evidence, especially when one witness kept calling repeatedly to say he was now seeing *two* of the creatures. It was twenty-six miles from Nowata to Noxie and after his initial investigations, the sheriff quit making the trip.

"I think after the first time, the witnesses were seeing and hearing ghosts." He added, "We're just trying to forget it."

About a month prior to the Noxie frenzy, Corona, California, Police Chief Joe Greer was beginning to relax. The town's panic had subsided. They had found a monster costume on the ground near the area where they had received one of the reports of the "Foothill Monster." The name of the six-foot adolescent said to have worn the costume was not released. The authorities did not press charges.

"What the heck, there's no law against being a monster," Chief Greer said. "But we can get along without it."

Although the fortunate discovery of that costume did stop the dozens of cruising cars, many of whose passengers were packing guns and out to get the critter, there was one problem with the convenient hoax solution: the costume did not fit the description of the monster.

MONSTER SIGHTINGS REPORTED TO POLICE

Corona police said today that over the past 24 hours, a number of area residents have reported sighting a huge ape-like creature that was first seen near Chase Drive east of Main Street two weeks ago. . . .

Two Corona residents, 18 and 20 years of age, told police last Tuesday they had seen the monster and it had chased them while they fled in their car. They said they first saw the animal a couple of weeks prior to that time. . . .

A Corona resident, Irene P. Rambo, told officers she saw the beast about 3 P.M. yesterday. It looked over a high patio fence in front of her apartment, she stated.

She described the animal as about 10 feet tall, half human, half ape, and covered with [black] hair. It had human-like teeth, she said.

She told officers that she grabbed her two-year-old son from the patio and locked herself and the boy inside the apartment. . . .

Henry Leppard
Corona Independent
August 15, 1975

The costume found was not hair-covered. Nor could it have created the illusion of being ten feet tall unless someone that height was in it. The face was a rubber mask of the horror-movie character, the Wolfman, with prominent fangs in evidence. Two long cylindrical metal pipes made up the dangling arms that ended in large gloves. Its hair was from a light-colored string mop, and a stuffed knapsack, presumably worn backwards, provided the bulk of a seemingly massive chest.

"When I saw that picture in the paper, I wanted to call the police and tell them they were wrong, that isn't what I had seen and the real monster was still out there, but I didn't,"[3] said the attractive but sober-faced young mother. She no longer allows her son to play alone on the patio. She feels that the creature she observed from the lower chest up standing against her six-foot-high redwood fence might have been after the child.

A ten-foot-tall, black, hair-covered monster getting into a housing tract in the city, in daylight, without being observed? Massive storm drains intersect the city of Corona, cement tunnels large enough for a six-foot-tall man to comfortably maneuver through with ease and without being detected. Something ten feet tall could also do it, by stooping over. One such underground storm drain emerges close to Irene Rambo's residence.

And what James Mihalko, thirty-six, and Ernest Palmeira, thirty-four, both serious, mature family men, witnessed one Sunday morning in August 1975 at the edge of the Main Street Canyon also didn't resemble the costume, which would later close the case on the "Foothill Monster."

For them it had begun as a lark. Hearing rumors about some animal in the woods and discussing it while they talked to each other over "ham" radio, they decided to take a look for themselves that Friday night.

Mihalko and Palmeira stood peering down at the old reservoir below them; all that remained of it was a flat area with a four-foot crumbling wall. To their left were cultivated citrus groves, now ripe with fruit. Behind the dry reservoir rose the rugged mountains of the canyons, closed off due to the extreme fire hazard. There isn't much to do on a Friday night in a small town and a lot of people had the same idea—to go on a monster hunt. More than twenty cars were jammed into the cul-de-sac at the end of Main Street. Many of the passengers carried weapons. Some joked. Around midnight, they all heard the sounds.

"It was like a steer or horse was running in panic

through the brush, breaking big limbs," James Mihalko, a well-built, ruddy-faced construction worker, said. "We figured maybe it was some kids down there in the dark, so two of the guys went down in there, stomping around in the brush. They didn't make half the noise that this whatever-it-was made."

Yet the excitement of the unknown and curiosity compelled the two men to return to the foothills the following evening. They didn't carry guns but had obtained a spotlight to enable them to see into the small grove of trees behind the reservoir wall. It was Saturday night and the end of Main Street was again crowded with monster-hunters and young lovers. Mihalko and Palmeira left to eat a leisurely dinner at a restaurant in town, hoping to outwait at least the juveniles who would eventually be responding to curfew.

Near 3 A.M. the men drove up the narrow road past the citrus orchards to the mouth of the Main Street Canyon. They were in luck. The area was deserted. Driving the few remaining yards to their destination with the car lights off, they quietly got out of the vehicle. The night was still.

"It was like everything was frozen. Usually you can hear all kinds of small animals and birds, but even the crickets weren't chirping," Mihalko, the outdoorsman, observed.

Their spotlight, a powerful motorcycle sealed beam, was capable of lighting an area of some forty yards wide and several hundred yards out. After standing silently in the dark for about twenty seconds, they switched it on.

The hair-covered form was crouched near the stone wall when the spotlight hit it. Oversized eyes glared a fiery red as the stooped figure looked at the source of light. Then it stood erect, a ten-foot-tall creature of unbelievable proportions, its body covered completely with shaggy hair described as "a dull black." Taking three immense strides, it reached the grove of trees and there it stopped for a moment, again to look toward those who were searching it out. The red eyes, even at that distance of two hundred feet away, were estimated the size of quarters. And then it made a chilling, high-pitched sound.

"It wasn't a breathing sound or a shriek. More like a whistle, a sharp sound like drawing a breath back through its teeth. He was *massive* and so was his head —about twice the size of any man's. When he turned to look at us, he didn't turn his head but turned his whole body."

Suddenly the two men became aware of a pickup truck that had pulled alongside of them. Two teenagers jumped out with a shotgun and aimed at the thing standing at the edge of the grove of trees. Mihalko and Palmeira dissuaded them from pulling the trigger. When they turned back to look at the creature, it was gone.

The construction worker was to interpret the creature's deliberate look at them as one of anger. His companion, Palmeira, of Portuguese descent, would believe something different.

"It was like we had disturbed it, like if you wanted to be left alone and somebody comes up to you on the beach and you turn around and say, 'Oh, the hell with it!' The way it looked at us, well, I feel it had more hurt in it than we had in just seeing it. It seemed to be lost or so depressed or lonely, it reminded me of a person out somewhere trying to forget its problems."

That was to be a later reflection, however, for both men, pale with fear, headed immediately for a telephone to call the police.

"They laughed at us like we were a bunch of idiots."

Still trembling, the insistent eyewitnesses called the police again, wanting someone to believe the incredible form of life they had seen. One patrol car was eventually dispatched, but the officer turned his vehicle around before reaching the cul-de-sac, telling the men a daylight search was more in order. Mihalko and Palmeira knew they would have to press the issue.

At an all-night restaurant, they drank coffee and together sketched a composite of the being's face so they would not forget any of the details. They both concurred on what they had observed: its teeth were even, humanlike; the nose was flat against a rather flattened face; the black hair grew low on its forehead, sweeping back from the face; if there had been a neck, it was obscured in the prodigious amount of hair.

Ernest Palmeira was experiencing a throbbing headache, a pressure he likened to "dropping a sponge in water and watching it swell." After the sketch was completed, the men parted, driving to their respective homes.

James Mihalko's pretty teenage daughter would later comment, "Daddy was super-scared when he came home that night. He told us to lock all the windows and doors and not leave the bedroom!"

After a sleepless night, the two witnesses went in person to the Corona Police Station that Sunday afternoon, to insist on filing an official report. The officer questioning them would say, "They told a most convincing story."

And Mihalko was convinced they had not overestimated the creature's height when one officer stood by the tree where the thing had turned to look at the two men, making that strange whistling sound. The witnesses were not allowed to join the police in their search around the old reservoir but watched the investigators from the observation point where they had stood staring at the hair-covered being. The figures below them looked half its size. The public was told that no clues or evidence had been found. There were no footprints. An aerial search of the canyons by Chief Greer and Detective Steve Evans revealed nothing.

The Mihalko-Palmeira sketch and story hit the local newspaper on Monday, August 18. On the following day, the costume turned up, along with the unnamed teenager confessing he had been the monster. At least three eyewitnesses do not agree with the official solution of a hoax. The Wolfman mask bore no resemblance to what they had seen, but they aren't making an issue of it. The real danger had never been with the monster, as far as they knew, but with the possibility of accidents occurring with the gun-carrying hunters who wanted to track down the thing. If the authorities wanted to brand their sightings the result of a hoax, that was all right with them. The witnesses knew otherwise. They would never forget.

Although Mihalko and Palmeira both saw the same ten-foot, hairy black form turn to look at them, their afterthoughts are dissimilar.

Ernest Palmeira: After the shock wore off and I started letting my mind slow down, I realized that the thing has human tendencies and it's got a problem. I'm more concerned about what's going to be done *for* it. I think that it could be communicated with.

The way it looked at us even now keeps preying on my mind. I keep seeing the eyes and the sadness in them. They seemed to lock in on me and I keep remembering, like it's embedded in a part of me that's making me *think* about it.

It was tremendous, huge in size, and we can't understand its action. I'm glad that it hasn't hurt anybody. I hope it doesn't get that way. I just keep feeling sorry for it. . . .

James Mihalko: I'm a hunter. I don't have the same pity that Ernie does. But God help the man that runs into that thing, because he wouldn't have a chance. If anybody's going to shoot it and he's close enough to shoot, it better be a lucky shot because they aren't going to get a second shot. As *quick* as that thing moves, it would be right on you. It's scary, strong, and could hurt.

I don't know if it's an animal or what but nothing ever scared me like this. I've had timber wolves come up and step around my feet and I've let them walk on by me. I've been faced with bears, and I know what a gorilla looks like, but this thing didn't look anything like a gorilla or anything like a man.

Law-enforcement agencies both in Nowata and Corona do not speculate on what "it" might be. They just want to forget the mushrooming panic they had to contend with and hope the monster doesn't come back. On a later check of possible updated reports, Sgt. Gary Salyer, Corona Police, said, "There is nothing new, thank God."[4]

While no footprints were found in the Oklahoma or California incidents, Game Warden A. C. Goodwin of Chatham County in North Carolina was coping with quite the opposite: one hundred three-toed footprints measuring some nineteen inches long—and no creature to go with them.

They were discovered September 10, 1975, making a trail across Mrs. Brodie Parker's acre garden. They led into the woods, which would thicken nearing Deep River.

"The biggest, ugliest tracks I've seen," commented Mrs. Parker.

While the Parkers were hoping that it was all the result of someone playing a prank on them, the evidence indicates otherwise. The toes seem to shift with different steps, the amount of mud between the toes differing from step to step, as it would if the "foot" was authentic. The stride measured a yard between prints, which passed the bean patch where, it was discovered, the tops of the beans had been pulled off. Unchewed, they had been thrown to the ground. Also, large limbs from pecan trees were found broken off, even though there had been no strong winds.

Prior to the finding of the three-toed prints, the Parker family dog was behaving strangely. "He was almost having a fit he was so scared. . . ."

The wildlife officer for the district was notified. So was the sheriff. The word about a monster got around fast and by the time the report had been made at the end of the day, an estimated two hundred people were at the Parker farm, armed with guns, looking at the tracks, and talking about going after the monster.

Something with three toes crossing the bean patch in huge strides was one thing; hundreds of trespassers was another. The Parkers plowed up the field and obliterated the tracks.

Warden Goodwin issued a statement that the foot-prints had been made by a prankster. But, he admitted, "If you were a game warden, you'd be saying the same thing—that it's a hoax—to keep those people from shooting each other."

Deputy Larry Harris didn't think it was a hoax. He had seen the prints and the broken limbs from the pecan trees. "I think it's for real."

The Parkers began to wonder if this was a routine path that the three-toed thing might be taking. "We found another footprint, an older footprint, just like the others, except it had some lespedeza growed up in it," Mrs. Parker would relate.[5]

She decided to follow the rather cryptic advice given her by her landlady ten years before when the family had moved in.

"She told me there were two and three hooks on every door—and to use them."

NOTES

1. *Arkansas Gazette* (Friday, Sept. 5, 1975).
2. *Corona Independent* (Tuesday, August 19, 1975).
3. *Op. cit.*
4. *Corona Enterprise* (Tuesday, August 19, 1975).
5. Bonnie Jordan, *Daily News* (Greensboro, N.C., September 19, 1975).

10

The Coincidence Factor[1]

My folks used to tell me of this legend which
was passed on to them by their parents about a
large man with red eyes who came to live with the
tribe. Whenever any of the Indian people became
sick, he would heal them. One day, when he knew
he was dying, he asked the Indian people to take
him to a particular location so that he might be
there when he died. This they did. Shortly after
he died, a large flying object came down from the
skies, put his body aboard, and flew off into the
sky.

As told to W. J. Vogel
by a Yakima Indian Fire
Guard, August 1974

The Yakima, Washington, Indians, like many other
tribes, have legends concerning flying objects and giant
people that they do not readily share with outsiders. In

maintaining silence, they avoid aggravating the general
skepticism in which many ancient Indian beliefs are
already held. Thus, they saw nothing remarkable when
the wire services excitedly announced Kenneth Arnold's
sighting of nine metallic, circular craft at nearby Mt.
Rainier in 1947—objects that would popularly become
known as "flying saucers." They knew of the sightings
of the hair-covered one they called the "giant" on that
mountain, dating back to the nineteenth century. It was
the white man who had to come to terms with these
things. For many years, the Yakimas had seen strange
lights over the reservation hills and down in the valleys.
They had glimpsed the large, foul-smelling creature the
white man called Bigfoot in their forests and around
their campfires. They didn't talk about it to outsiders.

An Indian logging contractor did attempt, in the early
1960s, to relate some of his encounters with UFOs to
Agency Forestry Department personnel, but no one
believed him. After being subjected to a lot of good-
natured ridicule, he simply quit talking about his experiences. This Indian (whom we'll call John Jay) and
his wife would drive through certain areas on the
reservation they knew to be prime spots for this aerial
phenomena and, for entertainment, watch the skies.

On one particular evening, the couple observed a
bright light hovering over a ridge in back of them as
they drove down a logging road near the Satus Peak
Fire Lookout. Thinking it might be watching them, the
Jays stopped their pickup truck and turned off the lights
—to see what the object would do. The UFO moved
in quickly, now hovering just several hundred yards
away.

Out of curiosity, Jay took out his flashlight and
blinked it at the object, hoping for a response. Then he
wished he hadn't. The bright, glowing craft instantly
maneuvered directly over their truck. The Jays decided
it was time to leave. The UFO continued to harass them
by making figure "S" turns back and forth over their
vehicle until they reached a more populated area in the
valley. Then the object turned, heading back in the
direction of the heavily forested region from which it

had come. The only noise the couple had heard was a slight humming sound.

On still another evening of sky watching around Toppenish Ridge, the couple noticed a reddish-white glow emanating from a depression to the side of the road ahead of them. Jay stopped the truck and they waited, watching the light, which was growing brighter and more intense.

"I got the overwhelming feeling that we were in danger and had better get the hell out of there," the Indian contractor said. His wife, already sensing the same threat, had slid to the floorboard in an effort to hide.

Driving out of the remote area as fast as possible, Jay turned around to see if this thing would also follow them, but to his great relief, it did not.

W. J. (Bill) Vogel, Staff Fire Control Officer, stationed on the reservation for more than twenty years, recently said, "Now I, for one, realize how right Jay was, but at the time none of us would listen to him."

The region within the Yakima Reservation out of which the majority of Bigfoot and UFO sightings are reported is rolling range country broken by deep, roadless, and almost inaccessible narrow canyons rising steeply into dense timberland. Volcanic Mt. Adams dominates the western skyline. On the west, the 1.25-million-acre reservation is bordered by the Cascade Mountain Range.

The Yakima Tribal Council maintains strict regulations, rigidly enforced concerning entry to reservation lands by non-Indians. And because this is an extremely hazardous fire area, no activity of any kind can be carried out by another governmental agency without the fire organization being informed.

It was only when Bill Vogel's own fire lookouts—all exceptionally trained and experienced observers—began reporting that they were seeing unusual lights and strange metallic objects, hearing subterranean noises and cries in the night sounding like the wail of a baby, that he became alert. ·

Vogel was not the kind of man given to speculation

or theories about "flying saucers." In his late forties, the well-built graduate from Washington State University had served as a division boss on the devastating Alaskan Swanson River fire in 1969, a fire that consumed 86,000 acres, taking 4,000 fire-fighters to bring under control at a cost of over fifteen million dollars. He was a man experienced in paying attention to "smokes," and although he didn't know what kind of "fire" all the UFO reports in the early 1970s indicated, he began a detailed compilation. While his documentation mainly concerned UFO sightings, he kept his ears open to a sudden influx of comments from the Yakimas about seeing large hair-covered beings.

A forester said he was walking through a heavily timbered area and was followed by "something" for a distance of three miles. When the forester (not an Indian) would stop walking, he could hear the heavy footfalls behind him quickly cease. The man tried circling but could not get a glimpse of whatever was following him. Unusual behavior for a cow. A cougar, perhaps, but these cats are usually silent and stealthy. He was accustomed to being in the woods alone and was not easily spooked. He knew that whatever was following him was something out of the ordinary. An Indian fire guard told Vogel that when he was riding his horse through the hills rounding up cattle, he came across some oversized, manlike footprints, which he followed. "He eventually caught sight of something that was large and very definitely not a man," Vogel said. "As he was by himself, he decided right then to forget the whole thing and quit following it."

Dorthea Sturm, Forestry lookout, works on a windswept rocky peak at an elevation of 4,180 feet at the Satus Peak Lookout. Below her are several heavily wooded canyons. She was to report that for two years she'd heard a spasmodic rumbling coming from the ground somewhere *beneath* the post. She wondered if it might be a dormant volcano. Described as sounding like "a logging truck pulling up a hill it never reaches the top of," it caused no vibration or shaking of the ground as would be expected if caused by underground slides.

And from deep within the dark, restricted canyons, "glows" were observed a number of times from two separate observation posts—lights looking like "a small city at night shining up out of the darkness." Yet this area is not accessible by foot or vehicle.

A former Satus Peak Lookout employee, stationed there for five years prior to Dorthea Sturm, stated he would not go back to that particular post for any amount of money. He and his wife had also heard the underground sounds, occasionally accompanied by a high-frequency noise that hurt their ears. Then there were those nights when the wails started, "like a woman screaming or a baby crying. . . ."

Vogel asked Dorthea Sturm if she had heard any similar cries. "She mentioned that the wind sure made some odd noises at times. I didn't pursue the subject as I didn't want to frighten her. I know she was most upset last summer [1973] when she found an ax handle laying by her outside stairway one morning when it wasn't there the night before. The soil around the lookout is all basalt so there would have been no tracks."

The Staff Fire Control Officer's files on the strange sightings that occurred throughout the reservation began to swell. Construction crews building a new lookout station reported that at dusk, just when they were leaving the site, three orange-colored "balls" came from the timbered canyons to the west, dropped down to just above the ground, and circled the new building several times as if inspecting the progress. Then they moved off, disappearing behind the hills. This same phenomena occurred when the microwave station was installed.

At times, Vogel would be alerted that a blaze was starting but would be baffled when he was unable to locate it. On one occasion, a lookout reported a huge fire burning in the shape of a column. The fire officer would again alert a team to start for the blaze, but before they could reach the area, the lookout radioed back that the fire had appeared to die down. The team along with a helicopter could not locate a trace of fire, smoke, or ground-scorched area, even though there had been a precise "fix" on the location. Equally puzzling were those areas where the brush appeared to have been burned and *no* fires were observed.

In the latter part of 1972, a Sopelia lookout reported a rocket-shaped object that flew out of the canyon directly in front of her. This was especially strange since she had been concentrating on that area and had not seen anything fly in!

In July 1974, a Satus lookout, intently watching through binoculars in the direction of Mt. Adams, where she had earlier observed a brilliant flash of light, saw a low-flying silver cigar-shaped craft come into view, skimming just over the treetops. It disappeared into a deep canyon known as the Middle Fork of Toppenish Creek. The lookout continued to watch, but the craft did not reappear.

This same lookout, checking the canyons for any possible "smokes" that might have started during the night, observed a bright round object hovering near the ground a short distance away. As she watched, two smaller and similar objects approached the larger one and either entered it or were absorbed by it. The larger craft then slowly moved off, going out of eye range beyond the mountains.

Vogel was himself to see and photograph some of the differently shaped and variously colored objects. The first was at 1:30 A.M. in August 1971 as he drove on US 97 toward Satus Pass to check for fires. Suddenly he noticed a large, bright, teardrop-shaped object above him.

"It was light tan around the edges, which were almost fluorescent. The brightness caused a halo glow around the object. I observed it through binoculars and then could see a mouselike tail at the top [the pointed end of the teardrop]. The tail was about half as long as the main object and seemed segmented in colors of red, blue, and green."

Later triangulation from three different locations by a licensed Forestry surveyor placed the craft at an altitude of some eight thousand feet. Its path was parallel to a main power-transmission line from the Bonneville Dam. Examination of Vogel's slides of the object by the Grizzle Observatory in Wenatchee, Washington, proclaimed the object definitely not stellar. The National Weather Service could offer no explanation; it was not a weather balloon, for they had none in the area at that time. The object was not shaped like any of their balloons, they said, nor would one reflect such intense light at that time of the night. Also, it was moving against the wind.

In the fall of 1972, Vogel would observe the scheduled Hughes Air West flight taking off from Yakima, climbing for altitude over the Horse Heaven Hills with a UFO making a right-angle course change and heading on a collision course toward it. Just before reaching the plane, the bright white light blinked out.

About this time, Vogel began to wonder if there were underground facilities in that region being secretly used by UFOs. In a letter to Dr. J. Allen Hynek at Northwestern University, he wrote, "Dry Creek, which heads in deep canyons south of Satus Lookout, disappears into the ground as it flows eastward. Trout marked and placed in the upper portion of the creek have been caught in the two lakes at the bottom of a large landslide on the north slope of the Toppenish Ridge. It is this same general area in which so many sightings have been reported and also from these same canyons that the lookouts have observed the emanation of the mysterious glowing lights. Could it be that there are subterranean caves throughout this area which are being used?"[2]

And as additional members of the Forestry Department began to pay attention to all reports of unusual aerial objects without ridicule, a few of the Yakima Indians hesitantly stepped forward to relate other things happening . . . about encounters with "the giant."

Two young Indians in their twenties had been out hunting on the reservation near Vessey Springs. Stopping their pickup to answer a call of nature, they heard the sound of something large running toward them down the gravel road. The apelike being was almost upon them before they were able to distinguish its features in the dusk. Thoroughly shaken by its appearance, they jumped into the truck and sped away. They reported that the "thing," running on two legs in hot pursuit, almost caught up to the truck before they accelerated and outdistanced it.

In 1972, near the North Fork of Logy Creek, a rancher in his early sixties watched in horror as a large, hairy being with an overpowering stench approached his cattle camp. It was apparently following his dogs. It stood on the edge of the firelight, looking at both he and his dogs for several minutes. The dogs did not bark. They were paralyzed with fear. Finally the immense foul-smelling creature turned, shuffling back into the surrounding brush and darkness. In the morning, the stench from the "thing" still lingered, making him sick to his stomach.

Vogel interviewed the rancher's employers. "They said he was a very truthful man and not one subject to making up stories or having fantasies. They did not believe he would fabricate such a story and said the Indian was upset and frightened while relating the incident to them."

Was this the same creature who approached the seven sleeping campers near Smith Springs that year? "They were awakened by a sound which they said they had never heard before—hair-raising. It was a sort of crying, growling type of sound," Vogel related. "It went on for most of the night, circling their camp. Even being hardened outdoorsmen, they were terrified. The group were well acquainted with the sounds of cougars and other forest wildlife. These sounds were something unique and unordinary."

Yakima legends tell of the Stick People. They say that, when they are sleeping in the woods, the Indians will awaken to see figures standing near them, but as soon as they begin to stir, the Stick People quickly fade out of sight, moving back into the forest. Is this simply folklore or figments of imagination? Are they ghosts, Bigfoot, or aliens?

While the lady wishes her name withheld due to the stigma of seeing "monsters," she is a mature and respected businesswoman who owns a tobacco store on the reservation as well as a large ranch. Her sighting occurred in the spring on 1963 while living at the base of Hambre Mountain on Toppenish Ridge. It was about 10:00 P.M. She sat reading while her husband slept on a nearby couch. Suddenly she began to feel uncomfortable, as if something was watching her. She glanced at the window, and an apelike face peered in at her quizzically, curiously.

It seemed to be kneeling at the window, for she could see the form from rib cage up. The window was four feet from ground level. The creature's girth filled the entire pane. The face, while not covered with heavy hair, was partially hairy, silky rather than coarse, the color of a golden or reddish cocker spaniel. Its nose appeared somewhat flattened; the mouth was humanlike, as were the teeth. The left eyelid drooped over amber-colored eyes, as if it had sustained a former injury.

Her screams awakened her husband, and with that, the face disappeared. Grabbing for his gun, her husband jerked open the door, puzzled by their normally good watchdogs, who had not barked and dashed through his legs in panic into the safety of the living room. Apparently the apelike being had fled into the brush-covered hills. Because of a mud problem, the yard had been covered with pea-sized gravel, making any identification of the creature's tracks impossible.

More sightings of UFOs, Bigfootlike beings, and underground sounds continue to filter across Bill Vogel's desk to date. As the subject of "flying saucers" becomes more respectable, its study being currently conducted by reputable scientific groups across the country, the Yakima Indians step forward to confide in the staff fire control officer—a man who will not laugh at them now—relating their encounters with the bad-smelling hairy "giant" seen in their forests, on logging trails, and at campsites. Still many of the Indians maintain a stoic silence.

No one can really determine at this time whether the two unusual phenomena are in any way related, even though the sudden influx of Bigfoot reports coincided dramatically with the increase of UFO activity. Perhaps it is simply because the "laughter curtain" was lifted.[3]

Or, perhaps, there might be something more tangible and interrelated in the coincidence factor if every incident were out in the open and available for statistical analysis. Would meaningful patterns emerge? Would we be able to determine what or who might be hiding in the unexplored canyons and subterranean caverns on the Yakima Indian Reservation . . . and why?

Bill Vogel has this to say, "While I have never had the frightening experience to encounter or see a Bigfoot, I have talked to enough persons I know are credible to realize these creatures are not figments of someone's imagination. What they are or where they come from or where they go, I do not know. But I hope to be able to continue assisting in research of the subject so that someday we all will know the full story of these beings."

NOTES

1. Portions of this chapter have been taken from "Gods From Inner Space," by B. Ann Slate, *SAGA* (January 1975), as well as personal correspondence with W. J. Vogel.

2. In 1971, W. J. Vogel contacted Dr. J. Allen Hynek, noted astronomer, former consultant to the Air Force's UFO investigations (Project Blue Book), and currently director of the Center for UFO Studies in Illinois. After appraising the high incident of repeated UFO activity on the Yakima Indian Reservation, Hynek sent scientifically trained observers with specialized monitoring equipment to the Toppenish Ridge area. Those findings were published in an article in *SAGA* (February 1975), "Operation UFO Stakeout," by B. Ann Slate.

3. "Laughter curtain" is a phrase coined by nuclear physicist-UFO lecturer Stanton T. Friedman, referring to the ridicule and derision many UFO eyewitnesses face when reporting a sighting.

11
Nature of the Quest: A Serious Game

The following story appeared August 11, 1973, in the Reno *Evening Gazette,* in a letter to the editor from Mr. and Mrs. Donald Cowdell and Mr. and Mrs. Charles Searles, all of Murray, Utah.

We recently visited Lake Tahoe for the first time . . . and while on our way up Kingsbury Grade, we had a very frightening experience.

It was about 8:30 P.M. July 29 [and we were] about two-thirds of the way up the grade, which you know is very narrow and steep.

As we came around a turn, we saw something on the side of the road which we thought was a black bear. As we got closer, it was standing on its hind feet in an upright position.

When it saw our car, it went into the bushes.

Just before it disappeared, it turned and looked at us.

Its face was more flat, like a gorilla's. It was about seven feet tall, and very shiny.

There was no place to get off the road, so we went on to Tahoe.

There were four people in the car and we all witnessed the same thing.

When we first saw it, my friend began yelling, "Blackfoot! Blackfoot! I mean, Bigfoot!" We don't know for sure what kind of an animal it was, but we do know we saw it.

In later interviews with the witnesses, more specific information emerged. The creature appeared to be crouching in a depression off the shoulder of the road when they first saw it. As their car drew near, it stood up on two legs and walked quickly away toward the cover of trees and brush. As the car passed and before the creature disappeared from view, it turned and looked back over its shoulder. It stood seven to eight feet tall, was heavily built, "big but not fat," and seemed well-proportioned except that the head was small.

It was covered with long, shiny black hair, which was thin on the chest and abdomen. Its face was flat and appeared leathery. Its eyes were round and dark, and glistened. It expressed no particular emotion but seemed observant and anxious to leave. It took long steps and had a smooth, swinging gait.

In recalling the incident, Charles Searles, manager of a business firm and an avid outdoorsman and hunter, remarked, "At the sheriff's office, they told us that there was a crazy Indian over in that area who had been dressing up in a gorilla suit and was trying to scare people. We just don't buy the idea. If someone had been trying to scare us, they would have liked us to know, they would have made gestures.

"This thing was trying to get out of our way. It was too natural-looking. There's no way that it could have been someone in a suit."

The Cowdells and Searles were certain of what they'd seen, and what they had *not* seen. Yet their observation of the creature was admittedly brief and the hour was shortly after sunset, when shadows deepen and dusk comes rapidly in mountainous terrain. Could they have been fooled by someone wearing an ape costume?

To explore that theory's merits, the authors first sought to determine the availability of such costumes by approaching major rental companies serving the motion-picture and television industry, then asked about the construction of a special realistic costume that might fool an unknowing observer.

We found that there is one Yeti costume available for lease in Hollywood, and that it is white, and that it would fool no one but the near-blind at several dozen yards. At Western Costume Company, the largest of the rental studios, numerous black gorilla suits are maintained. They are also offered in pink, blue, and beige, and for variety there is a selection of monkey suits in pastel colors. All patently designed for non-serious amusement. Nevertheless, as a test, we leased one of the suits and drafted a six-foot-four-inch-tall youth to try it on and go through some exercises.

"Take some giant steps," we said, whereupon the crotch of the suit ripped and the zipper was exposed.

The costume was characteristic. The arms were of average human length, not the reported nearly knee-length arms of a Bigfoot or of a real gorilla. The seat drooped conspicuously, lacking any special padding to lend the hindquarters a realistic effect. The chest was cut to human dimension, lacking either the space available or the padding to project great muscle and skeletal mass. The artificial fur glistened unnaturally. And our young actor's eyes never quite lined up in the eye sockets of the rigid, rubber head.

In short, it seemed inconceivable that the sight of anyone wearing such a suit could inspire much more than mild amusement or a knowing laugh, regardless of indoor or outdoor circumstances.

But what of a more costly, custom-made outfit tailored to an individual?

We consulted actor George D. Barrows, designer and inventor of the well-known NIGI gorilla costume, which is regarded as one of the most authentic gorilla suits ever made for use in motion pictures, television, and stage productions. Barrows tells of the time and effort that went into its creation.

Before I started constructing my costume, I researched data on the gorilla. This included reading about past living zoo specimens as well as gorillas that were alive in the various zoos around the world. I photographed Gargantua, the celebrated gorilla of the Ringling Bros. Barnum and Bailey Circus, and Toto, his mate.

I secured motion-picture footage on Mabongo and Nagigi, gorillas formerly residing at the San Diego Zoo. Bushman, the enormous French West African gorilla known the world over, who was in the Chicago Zoo, was also a subject of my studies.

A composite of all the aforementioned animals was used in the final modeling of the head. I also perused books and magazines to gather information about animals captured and shot by hunters and taxidermists of the caliber of Martin and Osa Johnson, Carl Akeley, W. K. Gregory, and others. I compiled a book with numerous photos and articles relating to the gorilla and his habits, and used this material as a background in designing, sculpting, and construction of the suit.

The actual costume was built by much sketching, drawings, and working out the proportions and scale size in relation to man and animal; this took a great deal of time and thought, involving the modeling of miniature animals to secure third-dimension proportions. I then built the head and face mechanism to allow articulation of the mouth, lips, nostrils, and eye areas.

The face and head were modeled in clay and a plaster of paris mold was made of it; the same was done for the hands, feet, and chest area. The body came next with the padding, body proportions, zippers, sewing, etc.

The most tedious effort was the ventilating—a

term used by wig makers which means the sewing in of the hair on all the exposed body areas of the costume. The hair used was a combination of Yak and Chinese.

To give the arms the tremendous length of the gorilla, extensions were built. These are mechanical hands which articulate from your own hands. The extensions add twenty inches to the arm span, which of course makes for great realism.

This, in a nut shell, about sums up the time, thought, and effort required to put together the NIGI gorilla costume. It was worth all the sweat and problems because over the years, it's proven successful and profitable.

I haven't touched on the acting or mime that requires this inanimate conglomeration of hair, rubber, and cloth to come alive and give the illusion of the real animal.

Would anyone go to such lengths to hoax a sighting of Bigfoot one summer's evening on Kingsbury Grade near Lake Tahoe? Who knows? We know of film footage and a few photographs depicting the creature that are alleged hoaxes, and we know that every so often in mountain communities where Bigfoot has become an issue, someone with a joke in mind dons big wooden "feet" and tromps around in the snow to harass researchers. But such pranks invariably are exposed for what they're worth (most often by the perpetrators), and the Bigfoot issue has not grown out of public concern over a few feet of fuzzy film and snapshots that seem deliberately out of focus. Hundreds of reliable witnesses have been involved, spanning dozens of years, covering thousands of square miles of sparsely settled wilderness territory. To account for the number of creatures described, numerous Bigfoot costumes of various sizes, shapes, individual features, and coloration would have to exist, presumably at the disposal of a supersecret sect of highly trained up-to-800-pound actors and mimes bent on fostering a myth and keeping it alive.

We think that a successful hoax is possible, given the

Barrows formula for realism, but as a final explanation for the widespread, historical phenomena, it is untenable—about as scientifically untenable and improbable as the creature itself.

The massive data collected, as well as hundreds of recent and reputable eyewitness accounts, indicate the alternative—Bigfoot exists. But how to prove it, even to satisfy one's personal curiosity, let alone arouse the interest of the public at large or a hidebound scientific community whose specialists and institutions are supposedly geared toward research and exploration of unknowns? In many ways it has seemed as if the proverbial deck were stacked. What do you do as a researcher when a forest ranger discovers you examining a fresh set of Bigfoot prints you've found in the wild, proceeds to destroy them with his boot while your back is turned, then warns you not to say anything to anyone about what you saw?

Do you just shrug your shoulders and forget about it? Or do you take another tack and pursue the investigation? The night of the Cowdell-Searles sighting on Kingsbury Grade, sheriff's deputies had treated the matter seriously enough to broadcast it over police radio bands and send a patrol car to the site. Without knowing this in advance from the contents of the letter published by the *Evening Gazette,* we made inquiries at a number of agencies in the South Tahoe area, including the South Shore Police Department; the Placer County, California, Sheriff's substation; and the Douglas County, Nevada, Sheriff's substation at Zephyr Cove. None admitted any knowledge of the incident. It was at the latter substation where the Cowdells and Searles had been told that the creature they'd seen was just a "crazy" Indian in an ape suit. Here's the line we got a few weeks later.

Deputy, responding, "Don't you realize that we have some of the world's greatest entertainers come up here? Why, just a while back, there was a four-hundred-pound actor who was playing the clubs at Stateline and he had a face just like an ape!"

Woman dispatcher, "That was two years ago, Harry. He ain't around here now."

Deputy Harry, "Well, maybe he came back. But even if he didn't, heck, I've seen lots of people around here that look like apes and gorillas."

Second deputy, chortling over the *Evening Gazette* clipping, "Now who the hell would ever tell anybody anything like that?"

It was at Markleeville in Alpine County, California, fifty miles south of Lake Tahoe, where we first learned of the radio broadcast by the Nevada sheriff's agency.

"It was all over the air that night," an Alpine County deputy recalled. "But I'm not surprised you didn't find out anything. All they're concerned about up there at Tahoe is bad publicity, anything that might hurt the gambling and entertainment business, the tourist trade. . . ."

With evidence and sometimes hard-won documentation at hand we have appealed to various individuals and institutions within the scientific community, thinking, as always, that they should be better equipped, better trained, and better funded to research and analyze the evidence and documentation, and do something about it. We assumed that there would be scientific interest, which may have been an error, and found that indeed the most usual response was no response at all.

There have been a few ripples, however. In one instance, Jane Goodall, widely publicized chimpanzee expert and visiting professor in psychiatry and human biology at Stanford University, was approached and asked for help in analyzing the Sierra creature vocalizations. The letter went out in December 1973. Ten months later, in October 1974, she replied, apologizing that somehow the letter had found its way into a batch of "antique" correspondence that only recently had been brought to her attention. She said that yes, indeed, she was interested in Bigfoot ". . . just as I am interested in the abominable snowman and other tales of red and hairy apes which are occasionally reported in various parts of Africa."

The letter was a delightful departure from past experiences and we pounced upon it, immediately drafting a reply intended to elicit a firmer response if not a promise of assistance. Allies of public standing in science are invaluable.

Our return letter outlined the Sierra story, referred to the limited analysis of the Bigfoot vocalizations taped there, and addressed the need for further "competent and willing hands" to determine their authenticity and scientific value. It dealt with the possibility of a hoax, noting that, even if one were established, the idea to conceive it had to have an origin, and that in itself might make a compelling subject for any student of human behavior. It dealt with the possibility that the sounds and evidence might represent precisely what they seemed to represent, ". . . the hairy form that it's cracked up to be." The letter also dealt with the observation that Bigfoot was a good story regardless whether it was real, or imagined, or the result of clever fakery, because it spoke of contemporary human needs, a condition and a state of mind. In its detail, it was meant to be circumspect and persuasive to a rational intellect, to appeal to one's sense of logic, fair play, and sympathy. In the end, key witnesses, the camp's location, and all but a paid vacation were offered. "Now, if this long letter is not enough," it began.

The long letter was enough. Several weeks later, Jane Goodall answered, "I am fascinated by the phenomenon and by your approach to the problem too. Again, I wish you the best of luck."

As setbacks go, it was mild enough. In mid-December, a year after our initial letter, we wrote again, asking directly if she might put us in touch with someone at Stanford's acoustics laboratory (one of two recommended by Syntonic Research, Inc.). When there was no reply by late January 1975, we offered her what we felt was our best shot, a demonstration record containing segments of the creature vocalizations and sound.

A few weeks after that we received a note from the Stanford Primate Research Group thanking us for the recording and informing us that Jane Goodall had gone to East Africa and would not be returning for a number of months.

We have learned not to be disappointed with the discovery that an effort has been misdirected or that any amount of guile and friendly persuasion has failed, even though sometimes it has taken weeks and even months for the message to sink in. Another letter was sent to the Research Group.

"As you must know something of [our] appeal to Dr. Goodall regarding the 'Bigfoot' recordings, is there someone of the Research Group who would be technically competent and willing to assist in an analysis of the original recordings and the Bigfoot sounds?"

In time, a response came back. "At this time I can not think of anyone in particular who might be able to assist you in an analysis of the 'Bigfoot' recordings. However, due to the interest and importance of such a project, I will certainly keep your request in mind and refer to you anyone whom I feel could be of assistance. Again, best of luck to you."

Months have passed, but we still keep such notes tucked away in correspondence files along with carbons of letters like those to Dr. Goodall. Who knows when a university-based researcher may call in the interests of science due to the interest and importance of a Bigfoot project!

A stacked deck? We don't think so, really. Yet in some ways the Bigfoot quest is taking on the aura of a card game among its participants. In many ways it might be likened to a game of progressive poker with no house limits. No house, in fact. And on the basis of the information we've gathered as of this writing and "reporter's instinct," we can only wonder what may become of it. For as openers become harder to draw, the stakes grow, and it becomes more difficult for the players to back out. There must be a last hand, of course, and someone must win. What will become of Bigfoot then?

Three years ago, when it first seemed that we might be holding a high hand with the Sierra creatures close by, we phoned the National Geographic Society's research funding committee to explore the possibility of obtaining some scientific assistance and a grant. We spoke with the committee's secretary, Dr. Edwin Snider, who informed us directly that the National Geographic Society wasn't impressed by Bigfoot evidence and probably wouldn't consider funding any project dealing with it. Never willing to let a good door be shut without a struggle, in joking desperation we asked Dr. Snider *what* evidence would impress the society. Would a body on its doorstep be of any help? It must have struck him as a grisly idea, for he replied haltingly, "Well, I don't think *that* would be necessary." Rather, he said, the opinions of several eminent and established scientists might suffice.

He was trying to be polite, but we already knew, and so did he, that no eminent and established scientist would risk his stature in this way without a body in hand. Even recently, with the announcement that "clear and conclusive" photographs have been obtained establishing the existence of the Loch Ness monster, we have heard the familiar strain echoing through halls like those of the British Museum, where scientists dismissed the evidence out of hand and announced they would not believe in the monster until they had a carcass.

The attitude is tragic. For if "Nessie" exists, like Bigfoot it must be a rare and endangered species vulnerable to extinction if carelessly exploited. Good photographs should be enough, enough at least to get laws on the books for the creature's protection and provide incentive for serious and carefully controlled scientific study.

As it is, today there are neither laws nor controls and seldom are there more than pseudo-scientific research efforts—scientists generally seem beside themselves about the silliness of the idea. Yet there is evidence that merits scientific attention, and there are many "believers" who are convinced that a pot of gold awaits whoever meets science's most lofty and unconscionable demand for a carcass.

Imagine the possible consequences of that initial carcass, especially as in the case of Bigfoot. Would there be enough pieces to go around? Every university and scientific institution worldwide would want a slice of the action: an ounce of viscera here, a length of entrail there, a bit of brain tissue, and so forth. But best yet, another body intact, so as to eliminate any competition for choice parts, in-house scientific rivalry, stealing, and substitution! Think of the demands that museums and zoos would impose, the circuses, the road shows, the entrepreneurs.

Certainly we are not the only investigative reporters to wonder about where the tracks lead; many others in the field have expressed similar mixed emotions, including veterans like George Haas and Peter Byrne, who have sought to discourage those who would attempt to kill or capture the creature.

Already, however, there are individuals and groups who have announced their dedication to these ends, who maintain gigantic steel traps in the woods, and who have vowed to kill the creature on sight. We were amazed recently to read of one investigator, a rare anthropologist no less, who reportedly wants the U.S. Army called directly in on the hunt. Can you imagine half the State of Washington defoliated?

Perhaps we need a "house" to play against; perhaps it's time that we had game rules and limits imposed. For very few of us regard the wager as altogether silly, and as surely as science scoffs at lesser evidence and God made us all gamblers, one of us is going to come up with the winning hand. Unless, we might hope, Bigfoot has winged heels or a sympathetic UFO looking out for him!

Appendix A
The Minaret Skull

In the course of traveling through the middle and southern Sierra Mountains to gather background material, Alan Berry met a physician, Dr. Robert W. Denton, from Bishop, California, who in August 1965, while on a backpacking trip near the Minaret Mountains, had recovered an unusual skull. The skull had been kicked up by a mule tethered in a boggy area. It appeared to be human to the physician, but unusual in its size, shape, and markings.

On August 26, 1965, after several inquiries among people he knew, the physician sent the skull to Dr. Gerald K. Ridge, pathologist of the Ventura County General Hospital.

On September 29, 1965, Dr. Ridge wrote in reply:

> The calvarium which you sent to me . . . turned into a rather interesting specimen largely by virtue of the unusual length of the skull as well as a very unusual development of the nuchal ridge in the occipital zone. This latter fact for a time had me thinking this must be the skull of some anthropoid species other than human, inasmuch as this amount of nuchal ridge development had not been observed by me.
>
> The upshot of the investigation was that I took the calvarium with me to the Department of Archaeology at UCLA where Dr. Herman Bleib-

160

treul and Dr. Jack Frost [Prost] examined the specimen.

Their conclusions were quite definitely that this is the calvarium of a young human, but that it represents that of an Indian, the remains vary probably having been in the matrix or adjacent area for many, many years. The nuchal ridge development had not been observed by either of them in their rather extensive experience and Dr.. Frost [Prost] offered the possibility that this calvarium had been used as a scoop or utensil which would rather effectively explain some of the thin characteristics in the frontal zone as well as some of the traumatic defects that·were present on the exterior surface.

The conclusions, therefore, are that this is the calvarium of a young, ancient Indian male with no indications of any medico-legal import. I left the specimen with Dr. Bleibtreul and received a receipt for it.

Both of the men . . . in the Department of Archaeology would be quite interested in having the area pinpointed where this calvarium was found. If it would be possible for you to send me some kind of map of the region in which this was found so that it could be marked, I would appreciate it and would transmit it to Dr. Bleibtreul. They indicated that, if there had been no archaeological investigation in that region for 10 years or so, they might be interested in seeking further Indian remains in that area. So you see one never knows what is going to arise out of what appears to be primarily a rather simple problem.

Thank you so much for the opportunity of working with this specimen. . . .

On October 8, 1965, Dr. Denton answered, saying that he would forward a map pinpointing the discovery site. He added:

"From what little I know of this area, no one has done any archaeological investigation of the region at all, let alone for the last ten years. The area is not frequented by very many people; in fact [we] had some difficulty finding some of the trail. . . ."

On December 10, 1965, the physician sent Dr. Ridge a map identifying the discovery site and reasserted his opinion that "no archaeological work has ever been done" in the area.

With this, the file on the Minaret Skull seems to have been closed. As of the time Alan met with him in August 1973, the physician had heard nothing more about the skull or about Bleibtreul's and Prost's interest in a dig.

On August 26, 1973, Alan spoke with Dr. Ridge. He said that he had no recollection of there being any further communication on the matter from either Bleibtreul or Prost. "As I recall, they were going to follow up," he said.

In his talks with Alan, Dr. Ridge recalled the skull as "a rather massive piece of bone" of "peculiar shaping" and wondered, after eight years, what had become of it.

The following day, Alan contacted an anthropologist at the University of California at Davis and asked if he might help locate the skull through colleagues at UCLA, as Alan had already contacted officials there and they had disclaimed any knowledge of it. Alan mentioned that he was a reporter following up on a Sierra Bigfoot story, and he cited Dr. Ridge's remark about wondering if the skull was of "some anthropoid species other than human."

On September 10, 1973, Alan received a note from the anthropologist thanking him for a copy of Dr. Ridge's letter, advising that he had been in touch with friends at UCLA and had "no luck" in locating the calvarium, and that he was writing Dr. Bleibtreul at the University of Arizona at Tucson.

On October 9, 1973, Alan called the anthropologist, who told him that Dr. Bleibtreul had answered his queries: "He wrote a very short note saying, 'Hello, I'm sorry but I don't remember it.' He has no record or recollection of the skull."

After that, Alan contacted a museum technician at UCLA's Department of Anthropology. After hearing nothing from him, he then contacted an anthropologist there, again citing Dr. Ridge's observations about the unusual size and shape of the skull as reason for finding out what had become of it, recovering it, and possibly having it reexamined in light of new technology. That was December 7, 1973. On December 18, the UCLA anthropologist, Professor Clement Meighan, replied:

> Thanks for the copy of Dr. Ridge's letter. I have consulted with our museum technician [Clay A. Singer] and he has conducted a massive search of the records and collections without any success so far as your skull fragment is concerned. Apparently the specimen was never turned in to the museum for cataloging; if it had been, we would have a record of it. There is one last place we can check, and then Singer will send you a letter with whatever information we can find.
>
> I'm sorry we don't seem able to find this skull, but this is the first I have heard of it and it never came into any collections I have supervised. Possibly Bleibtreul or Prost took it with them when they left UCLA. . . .

Three weeks later, Clay A. Singer, the museum technician, wrote:

> I am sorry for taking so long to respond, but I have tried to be as exhaustive as possible in attempting to locate the skull fragment. I have personally questioned everyone in the department who might know something about it, including former museum technicians as far back as 1964. Nobody has seen it since mid-1965 when Prof. Prost had it in his lab. I have also carefully checked every burial and accessioned skull in our collection without result. It appears that it was never accessioned (i.e., given an official UCLA Museum number) and may have been taken back east with Dr. Prost when he left UCLA in 1965 or 1966. Anyhow, that is the only avenue that I have been unable to check carefully. . . .

I hope that Dr. Prost can do something about this question, and meanwhile I will keep a careful look-out for a skull that fits the description. . . .

Alan located Dr. Prost at the University of Chicago in Illinois and phoned him. He stated, flatly, that he had no memory of anyone ever giving him a skull—of any kind—while he was at UCLA, or of having such a skull in his lab there!

More than six months had passed since Alan's initial inquiry. He had been in touch with all the principal parties who had handled the unusual specimen and might know what had become of it, including Bobby Joe Williams, a museum technician who had worked with Dr. Bleibtreul at the time. On January 25, 1974, Williams told him, "Any material given to us was given to Archaeological Survey [a separate departmental office] or the Museum. I don't recollect anyone ever giving a skull of any kind. I'm sure if Herman Bleibtreul took the skull, he put it somewhere. I know Herman, and I know he would have labeled and stored it somewhere. He wouldn't have taken it with him unless he felt it wasn't significant enough to label and store. . . ."

Alan said that, according to Dr. Ridge, the skull was left with Dr. Bleibtreul and that he himself had received a receipt for it. Alan asked what the receipt, also missing, meant.

"The receipt means that he [Bleibtreul] wanted to put it in a collection . . ." Williams answered.

Alan phoned Dr. Bleibtreul, then dean of the Department of Anthropology at the University of Arizona. Dr. Bleibtreul had already written a professor at the University of California at Davis saying that he had no memory of the skull. Alan read Dr. Ridge's letter to him, and his memory was suddenly refreshed. He did indeed remember the specimen, he said. "It was certainly unusual. It was a peculiar thing—its morphology and markings."

Alan explained to the dean his hopes of finding the skull to have it reexamined and reappraised. He said that a search had been conducted at UCLA without success and that he had talked with Dr. Prost, but that Prost disclaimed any knowledge of the skull. He also asked if any search for the remainder of the skeleton or other skeletons in the Minaret area ever was conducted.

Dr. Bleibtreul said that, as he recalled, a search had been considered but had never taken place because they never received any information as to where exactly the skull was discovered!

He said that he was certain the skull had been catalogued and was still in the collections somewhere at UCLA. Now that he recalled it, he said, his own curiosity was aroused and he would like to have a look at it again and have it examined by a forensic expect. He said that he had some ideas about where it might be located in the museum collections, would write to UCLA, and see what he could do.

Four months later, on May 22, 1974, the dean and Alan talked again. He said that he was disappointed and sorry, but he'd had no success.

"It makes me angry," he said. "Things like that shouldn't be lost."

Ancient Indian, or an "anthropoid species other than human"? Dr. Bleibtreul noted that one of the problems he and Prost originally had in identifying the specimen was that, while they felt it must be aboriginal, it didn't fit any of the known populations from that area.

Can the observations of two anthropologists and a pathologist, all experts who were puzzled at the time by the skull's extraordinary, virtually subhuman characteristics, be dismissed as idle speculation? Lamentably, the specimen and all records of it, save those of a Bishop, California, physician, seem to have been lost or mislaid and the mystery will never be solved, until the skull or another one like it is rediscovered.

Appendix B
The Bigfoot Tapes

In early November 1973, after months of attempting to locate and enlist appropriate scientific aid in the analyses of the Bigfoot tapes, Alan Berry phoned I. E. Teibel, president of Syntonic Research, Inc., in New York City. Teibel recently had appeared on a nationally syndicated television talk show discussing former President Nixon and the Watergate tapes, the relative ease in altering tapes and the relative difficulty in detecting such alterations. Teibel had suggested on the talk show that his firm was experienced in exposing tapes that were hoaxes. Therefore, it seemed reasonable to expect that through him Alan might get to the bottom of the creature-sound mystery. For a fee, anyway,

He agreed to listen to a copy of the sounds, and on November 11, a copy was sent. In a covering letter, Alan wrote:

"I understand that you can't make any guarantee about proving or disproving [the tape's] authenticity. My hope is that you can help me build a case one way or another, however, or at least provide some basis for probable best interpretation where there remains a question mark. . . ."

Less than a week later, on November 16, Teibel wrote back:

"We have examined the tape copy you sent us on November 11th, utilizing the highest quality ¼-track

166

stereo playback equipment obtainable. A spectrum analyzer and a dual trace oscilloscope were also attached in the signal chain, so that visual analysis could be obtained simultaneously. Our findings are as follows. . . ."

The sounds were undistorted, he said. He also said that they had "a fairly high low-frequency component," and suggested that because of the power necessary to transmit low-frequency sounds, the source could not have been more than thirty feet away from the receiving microphone. The volume and "color" of the sounds remained relatively stable, he said, which indicated that the creature, assuming it was a creature, had not moved about while producing the sounds. He further said that the sounds were "almost completely localized on the right channel" (original recording was in stereo), which could only happen if the tape recorder's transducer malfunctioned or "the sound source was *very near the microphone*" (Teibel's emphasis). He added that there were "unmistakable" mike-handling noises and indications of tape-drive interruptions that led him to believe the recording was not continuous in nature.

"Since we do not have access to the original recording," Teibel continued, "our findings are based on the copy provided. . . ."

Alan had not forwarded the original tapes pending his report on the copy. Until their probable value was ascertained, it seemed foolish to risk their possible loss or destruction, either in the mail or as a result of careless handling. After reading Teibel's report, Alan knew that Teibel was in error about the continuous nature of the recording.

On November 20, 1973, Alan mailed off two of his original cassettes, along with a letter detailing the time, place, and circumstances under which the recordings were made. "From your analysis," he wrote, "it seems possible that one of the tapes [on the two dates in question, Oct. 21 and 22, 1972, separate recordings were also made by Warren Johnson, Bill McDowell, and Ron Morehead that were partial and noncontinuous in nature, and Alan had offered these to Teibel as soon

as they could be obtained] may have been a master pre-
recorded elsewhere then amplified from somewhere in
the immediate vicinity out into the woods. I want to explore this possibility."

It was the only possibility that seemed plausible to me,
given Teibel's preliminary findings; and if the evidence
were truly there, on the original tapes, it would be a
clear-cut indictment of Warren's group, and the authors'
gullibility. In still another letter, Alan provided more
details about the camp scene and circumstances. Perhaps out of frustration, realizing that more than a year's
investment in time, effort, and research of the phenomen
was at stake, Alan added a paragraph about the night
Larry Johnson and he had listened to the Old Man sing
his swan song.

"The point in drawing this picture for you is, would
a hoaxer subject himself to such conditions all night
long . . . in a remote wilderness setting, without knowing
or having any way to know whether the persons he was
hoaxing were awake and paying attention? Try to
imagine yourself there as I was, half frozen . . . in a
crude lean-to shelter, in fairly dense woods, at about
8,500 feet in late October after the first snowfall, some
2,000 feet higher than the nearest road and about eight
miles distant from the nearest established trail. Is this
setting alone constant with the idea of hoax, either
inside or outside this small group of people which had
been documenting similar experiences nearly to the
point of boredom for more than a year before I met
them?"

On December 6, Alan received a letter from Mike
Kron, one of Teiber's research associates, whose remarks now pertained to the original recordings:

We have played both tapes. . . . In my opinion,
the sounds recorded have been spontaneous in
nature and seem to have taken place at the time
of the original recording. There are some ques-
tionable clipped delay times at the end of certain utterances, and the recordings themselves are
not of the highest quality, due to the extreme con-

ditions under which they were made and the technical limitations of the microphone and tape recorder utilized. This thereby limits the amount of analysis that can be performed, as we do not have a standard-reference model for comparison, as would be the case with voice-print spectrograms.

I must state that the frequency range of the utterances could be considered humanoid and that these sounds could have, theoretically at least, been produced by a human adult male. We are not saying that this is the case, however.

Tape recordings are extraordinarily flexible and subject to all sorts of artful manipulations. The fact that a photograph of the beast supposedly on this cassette recording was not made limits the credibility of the recording. If you wish us to prove 100 percent that such a recording is either "fake" or "genuine" we cannot do either. Just as a recording of a "Martian" could only be analyzed by speculation. We have attempted to contact a zoologist here in New York who might wish to comment on these recordings but have been unable to do so as yet. . . .

I would suggest approaching a nearby engineering university for the detailed analysis these tapes require.

Kron's letter was accompanied by one of Alan's own, sent earlier to Teibel, in which Alan had presented a number of specific questions. Here are some of Teibel's notations and remarks.

Had the Bigfoot sounds come from a hidden amplifier?

T: "Interchanges are interesting—seem spontaneous —no obvious defects in sound although it *could* be from speaker."

Was there any sixty-cycle "hum" evident, which would indicate indoor prerecording?

T: "No hum evident from external source."

Was the source in fact "very near" the microphone,

as suggested by the preliminary analysis of the duplicate tape?

T: "Equalization in re-recording [the copy Alan had initially sent] changed emphasis somewhat. Original [tape] does not seem to indicate close recording."

What was the frequency range of the sounds?

T: "Basic freq. 200-2K Hz. Screeches much higher [5K]."

What is a human's range?

T: "App. same."

What is a gorilla's range?

T: "Lower range—1 more octave."

Teibel's final comment: "Get a picture!"

On December 14, 1973, Alan received a letter from Teibel:

We have attempted to interest various local scientists in examining the tapes you have provided. To this date, we have been in correspondence with several people who we thought might have interest in pursuing this matter on the basis of scientific interest alone. As we have been unable to obtain any positive response, and a week has passed, we are herewith returning the four tape cassettes [including one from Warren and one from Ron that Alan had sent] you have provided. . . .

My suggestion as to your further course of action would be to contact scientists closer to your locality, as verification based on tape analysis is extremely fragile, especially in light of the limitations of most tape cassette recording equipment and the absence of corroboration, either by photographic means or an expert witness.

Once you meet such a person, we feel you will be able to provide spontaneous data which will be helpful in examining this material and other material you might have. I would also suggest the following chain of activities: have a zoologist review the tapes in your presence; have him comment, in writing, on his observations; then submit the recordings and as much corroborative material as possible to a university acoustics laboratory which might undertake a *thorough* examination on the basis of scientific interest.

ABOUT THE AUTHORS

B. ANN SLATE, a native of Southern California, attended the University of California at both Santa Barbara and Berkeley. Her twenty years of research into UFOs, psychic healing, paranormal phenomena and the Sasquatch have taken her across the globe and into contact with the world's foremost authorities in these fields. She has been published in over fifty national and international magazines and newspapers. This writer-researcher maintains extensive files on these subjects, and numerous field trips and expeditions have led to firsthand encounters with the Bigfoot of northern and southern California.

ALAN R. BERRY was born January 17, 1941, in Glendale, California. His early childhood was spent largely in southern California, including summers in a boardwalk "tent city" at Huntington Beach, where he learned to swim, fish and hunt the elusive sand crab—all skills that he considers essential today for anyone taking up the pursuit of Bigfoot. Early exposure to camping and trout fishing in the High Sierra gave him a lasting affection for the mountain wilderness. He received a B.A. in English from San Francisco State College in 1963, and served as an artillery officer in Vietnam. He was honorably discharged in 1967, enrolled in law school for a year, became a state legislative aide for another year and finally, in 1969, entered journalism. Mr. Berry has traveled widely but prefers being close to California's mountains and beaches.

Hair-raising happenings
that guarantee nightmares!

You'll be fascinated by unearthly events, intrigued by stories of weird and bizarre occurrences, startled by terrifying tales that border fact and fiction, truth and fantasy. Look for these titles or use the handy coupon below. Go beyond time and space into the strange mysteries of all times!

PSYCHIC WORLD

Here are some of the leading books that delve into the world of the occult—that shed light on the powers of prophecy, of reincarnation and of foretelling the future.

Bantam Book Catalog

It lists over a thousand money-saving bestsellers originally priced from $3.75 to $15.00 —bestsellers that are yours now for as little as 60¢ to $2.95!

The catalog gives you a great opportunity to build your own private library at huge savings!

So don't delay any longer—send us your name and address and 25¢ (to help defray postage and handling costs).